MY NEW COMPUTER

A gentle introduction to your computer, the cloud, and the Internet

CYNTHIA M. NIKOLAI, PhD

One Printers Way
Altona, MB R0G 0B0
Canada

www.friesenpress.com

First Edition — 2024

ISBN
978-1-03-830374-5 (Hardcover)
978-1-03-830373-8 (Paperback)
978-1-03-830375-2 (eBook)

1. COMPUTERS, COMPUTER LITERACY

Distributed to the trade by The Ingram Book Company

Table of Contents

Introduction

Welcome to your new computer guide! This book is a gentle introduction to computers. In these pages you will learn about computers, the Internet, the cloud, privacy and security, and social media. This guide is intended as a discussion of the general what-is concepts of any computer rather than a guide on the ins and outs of the operating system. In some cases, where appropriate, I include a few basic how-to operations. You can always Google how to perform additional actions that you are interested in for your particular operating system. Each chapter consists of a discussion of key concepts followed by a set of exercises to apply your new knowledge. This guide is designed around the Windows 11 operating system.

I hope you enjoy and get a lot out of this book.

Cindy

Chapter 1: Where to Begin

In this chapter, we discuss what a computer is and how to navigate around the computer using a trackpad and mouse.

What Is a Computer?

A computer is a tool that stores and processes data, runs software applications, and performs calculations. A computer generally consists of a central processing unit (CPU), a fan to cool the CPU, a hard disk on which to store data, RAM on which to store additional data with faster access than a hard drive, and a set of peripherals (e.g., monitor, printer, scanner, mouse, keyboard, and headset).

Using a Trackpad or a Mouse to Navigate

A *trackpad* is the large square at the bottom of the keyboard on a laptop. There are two main functions on a trackpad or a mouse, the *left click* and the *right click*. A left click is where you use one finger, usually your index finger, to tap or click on the lower-left corner of the trackpad. It's called a left click because it's also the left button on your mouse. A right click is where you press two fingers at the same time on the lower-right corner of your trackpad. Sometimes there are buttons on the trackpad itself that allow for a left and right click (see Figure 1). Otherwise, imagine left and right buttons in the spots in Figure 1 in orange on your trackpad, and use those areas to perform left and right clicks.

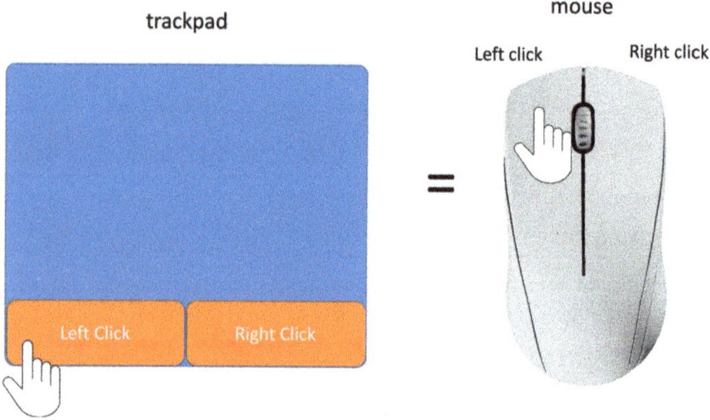

Figure 1: The left click on the trackpad (left) and mouse (right)

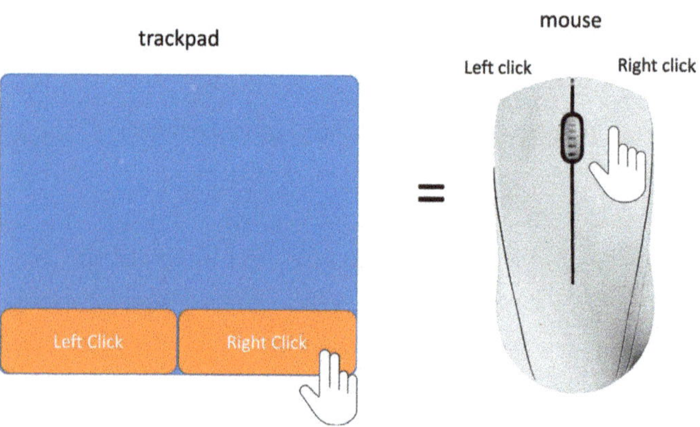

Figure 2: The right click on the trackpad (left) and mouse (right)

Right clicks usually show you menus, and left clicks usually allow you to select something or to perform an action. Ninety percent of the time, you will use a left click. When you want to see what options are available in a menu, use a right click. With a mouse, use the left button to left click and the right button to right click.

The Double Click

To double click on something, tap your finger on the left click area twice as quickly as you can.

Additional Fundamental Gestures

Trackpads allow for additional gestures—scroll, pinch, and reverse pinch. To *scroll*, place two fingers in the center of the trackpad, and then slide your fingers up and down on the trackpad. This will move the screen contents up and down so that you can see additional content. Some mice have a wheel protruding between the left and right buttons. To scroll with a mouse, use your index finger to rotate this wheel. (See Figure 3.)

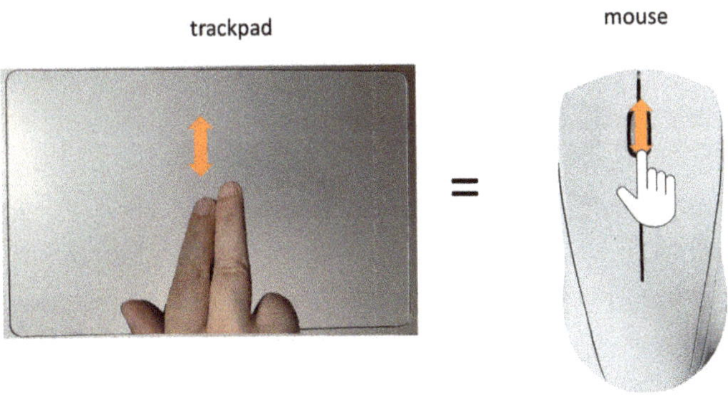

Figure 3: The scroll on the trackpad (left) and mouse (right)

The *pinch* is used to enlarge the screen's view, and the reverse pinch is used to make the view smaller again. To use a pinch, spread your thumb and index finger, then place them on the trackpad and then bring them together, as if pinching something.

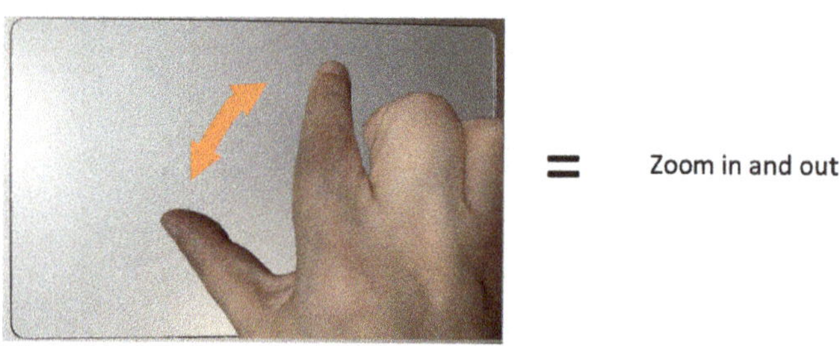

Figure 4: The pinch

The *reverse pinch* is just the opposite. Start with your thumb and index finger together and place them in the middle of the trackpad. Then slide your thumb and index finger apart, as if you are undoing the pinch. A pinch allows you to zoom in on a window. A reverse pinch allows you to zoom out of a window. A reverse pinch is also known as *pinching out.*

How Do I Connect to the Internet?

In Windows 10, click on the icon in the lower right-hand corner of the screen. In Windows 11, click on the icon. On a Macintosh, the icon is on the toolbar in the upper-right corner of the screen. Once you click on this icon, you will see a list of networks. Select a network and click on "Connect." Some networks are password protected. If your network is password protected, it will ask you for a password. Enter the password and then click "connect." This will connect you to the network, and you will have Internet access. When you connect to a network without physically connecting your computer to a router or modem with an ethernet cable, it is called Wi-Fi.

Tip: How do I get the network name and password? If you are in a public place such as Barnes and Noble or Starbucks, ask the store for the name of the network and the password, if required. If you are at home, ask your internet service provider.

~

Exercises

Exercise 1:
After you login to your computer, you should see your desktop (See Figure 5 in Chapter 2). Choose an icon, and double left click on it. It should open the associated program. To close it, click on the X in the upper-right corner.

Exercise 2:
After you login, you should see your desktop. Choose an icon, and double right click on it. You should get some menu options. Hit "ESC" on the keyboard to exit the menu.

Chapter 2: The Operating System

This chapter provides an overview of the operating system and the main interface that users use to interact with the computer. After this, it delves into the Windows 11 desktop.

The Operating System

An *operating system (OS)* is a system for organizing, accessing, and coordinating *applications* and *data* on a computer. Several operating systems are in use today. The one with which you are probably most familiar is Windows. Windows was created by and is owned by the Microsoft Corporation. Common versions of Windows are Windows 10 and Windows 11. Apple also has an operating system for its computers, called OS X. A third OS is ChromeOS, which was created and is used by Google on its Chromebook computers. Finally, there are *open-source* operating systems, which include the likes of Linux, RedHat, and Ubuntu.

When you turn on your computer, start by logging in, which will take you to the desktop.

> **Note**: sometimes a computer is configured to log you in automatically.

Desktop Overview

Your *desktop* is the main screen you see when you log in to your computer. A desktop is an intuitive way for users to interact with the computer using concepts that are similar to those used when interacting with the physical world, such as buttons and windows. It typically consists of icons, windows, toolbars, buttons, and wallpapers. The desktop is the main place on the computer where you will interact with it. The desktop on each OS is slightly different, but there are some common features that we will discuss.

First, you will have a space on the desktop for icons or shortcuts to common programs or files that you use. Second, you may have a mashup of news, photos, and weather, called the newsfeed. This is usually located on the task bar at the bottom of the screen. You will also be able to access your installed apps, turn your computer on and off, power down your computer, or put it in sleep mode. These functions can be accessed from the taskbar at the bottom of the desktop. Finally, there are additional apps, such as a calendar, as well as apps that show you the status of items on the computer, including how much battery charge is left (if using a laptop), if you are connected to the Internet, what the volume is set at, and the date and time.

The Desktop (Windows 11)

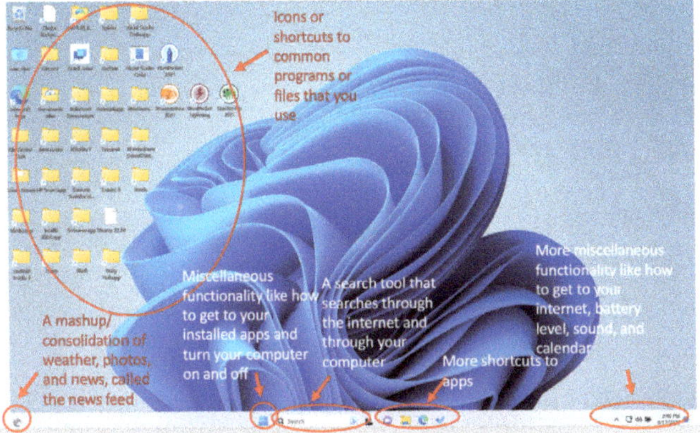

Figure 5: The Windows 11 desktop

Desktops provide a "drag and drop" capability that allows you to move icons and toolbars from place to place on the desktop or in the file system. It also allows you to drag and drop files and folders to different locations.

Once on the desktop, you can perform file operations, use an application, or configure the operating system.

Settings

An operating system can be configured in many different ways. For example, you can configure the file system to show file extensions in the File Explorer. To configure the OS, you will interact mainly with the Settings panel. The Settings panel is usually represented by a gray cog-wheel.

Here settings are grouped into common operations. Some common settings include:

- Accessibility

- Make screen text larger
- Add or remove printers
- Install or uninstall applications
- Keep windows up to date

> **Note**: there are many additional settings that you can use to customize your computing environment.

Automatic Updates

When an operating system first comes out, it usually contains *bugs*. As more and more individuals use the system, people report the bugs to the OS creator, and they are fixed. Sometimes bugs are reported automatically by the computer. Then an OS update is released. Operating systems such as Windows 10, Windows 11, OS X, and Linux have an automatic update feature. These software updates, also known as patches or fixes, correct bugs and fix security issues in the operating system to prevent hackers from stealing sensitive information from your computer or deleting or modifying files.

> **Tip**: Configuring your computer to automatically update its operating system will ensure you don't miss important security updates and bug fixes, which will help reduce the risk of your computer being compromised.

Tips

There are many options and features on a computer, so many that it can be overwhelming to try to learn them all at once. One tip for learning about your operating system is to use the Tips feature. This feature gives you bite-size tips about how to use your computer.

To access the Tips feature, search for tips in the windows search bar.

> **Tip:** A computer is a complex system. There is so much to learn, and it's nearly impossible to learn every aspect of the operating system and its accompanying software applications. Be gentle with yourself. Learn as much as you want to, but don't concern yourself with trying to learn every aspect of the computer or the Internet. The only thing constant about computers is change. Operating systems and software applications change frequently. Be prepared to revisit/relearn software as bug fixes, security fixes, and new features come out.

Windows Overview

Windows is a *graphical user interface (GUI)*. This means that you can interact with the computer through "windows" (See Figure 6).

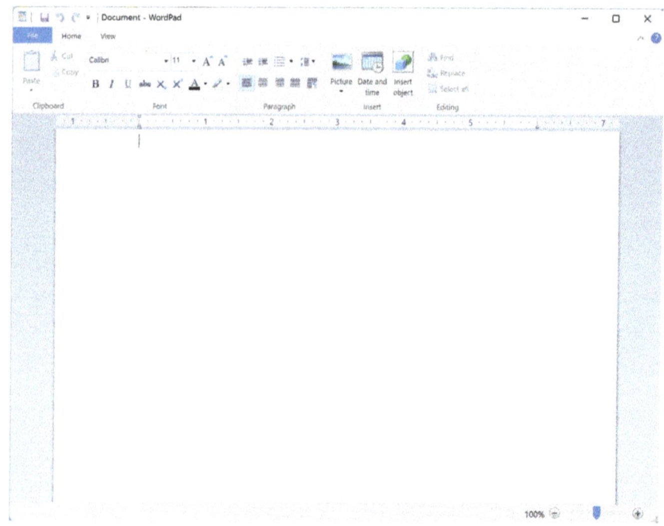

Figure 6: A typical window

There are two main parts to every window. The content is displayed in the center of the window. In the upper-right-hand corner, you will see a set of three symbols: – □ × . The – "minimizes" the window. That is, it leaves the program open and running in the background, even though it's not visible. When a window is minimized, it goes onto the taskbar as an icon with a tiny blue bar beneath it. You can access the program again by clicking on the icon on the taskbar. This will bring the program back into the foreground of your screen. The □ "maximizes" a window. That is, it makes the window take up the entire screen. When you maximize a window, the icon changes to a ⧉ icon. Clicking on the ⧉ icon returns the window to its original size. The X symbol closes the window and stops the file or the program from running on your computer. You can resize a window by hovering your cursor over the side, top, or bottom of the window until the cursor changes to a double arrow. Then left click and hold down your left finger and move your finger on the trackpad, or the mouse, left, right, up, or down until the window is the size that you want it. Then lift your finger and let go of the mouse/trackpad.

~

Exercises

Exercise 1:
Turn up the volume on your computer. (Hint: the volume is in the lower right-hand corner of the taskbar.)

Exercise 2:
Increase the size of the text on your screen. (Hint: text size settings are in "Settings" under "Accessibility.")

Exercise 3:
Make your mouse pointer larger. (Hint: mouse size settings are in "Settings" under "Accessibility.")

Exercise 4:
Go through the taskbar from left to right, and left click on each item. Observe what happens and what icons open which programs. (The goal of this exercise is for you to get more familiar with the desktop and all the icons on the screen). Remember, you can close a program by clicking on the X button in the upper-right-hand corner.

Otherwise, hit "ESC" or click anywhere outside the menu window to return to the main screen.

Chapter 3: What Do You Do with a Computer? (Checking Email)

In this chapter, we discuss how to set up and access your email.

Email Providers

To access email, you need to use an email provider. Several email providers are on the market. Some are free, and some you must pay to use. Although many email providers are free, they only allow a certain amount of storage. After you reach your quota, you will have to pay for additional storage.

Here are some of the free* email providers:

- Yahoo.com (owned by AT&T)
- Hotmail.com (owned by Microsoft)
- Gmail.com (owned by Google)

*Google Accounts come with 15 GB of cloud storage, which is shared across Google Drive, Gmail, and Google Photos. Yahoo accounts come with 1 TB of free storage. Hotmail accounts come with 15 GB of email storage space. Microsoft 365 subscribers get 50 GB of space.

Some email services are part of the service that your *Internet Service Provider (ISP)* provides. Examples include:

- att.net
- sbcglobal.net
- comcast.net

How Can I Access My Email?

There are three main ways to access your email. First, go to the service provider's email website interface, and access it online. For example, the Gmail access point is mail.google.com or gmail.com. The second way is through an *email client.* An email client is an application that allows you to access your email on your computer without going through a website. An advantage of using an email client is that you can access multiple email accounts in one location. For example, you can access your Gmail account, your Comcast account, and your Hotmail account in one convenient location. Email clients also have more advanced features than online email portals.

Example email clients include Microsoft's Outlook and Apple's Mail. A subscription for Office 365 is required to access Outlook, although a simple free version comes with the Windows OS.

To set up your email account for access through Outlook, go to the "File" menu and then "Accounts," and add a new email account. Follow the on-screen instructions. If you are unclear about how to do this, ask your email provider how to set up your email in an email client.

The third way to access your mail is through a cell phone or tablet. Ask your cellular service provider to guide you through the setup process.

~

Exercises

Exercise 1:
Open your email through a web browser. (Note: if you are not familiar with web browsers, then do this exercise after you read Chapter 6: Web Browsers.)

Exercise 2:
Open your email with an email client (e.g., Outlook). (Note: you will have to set up your email in the client before you can use it. Reference Chapter 3: How Can I Access My Email?)

Chapter 4: What Do You Do with a Computer? (Storing and Retrieving Data)

This chapter discusses files and folders. We begin with what a file is and common file types. Next, we delve into how to access files and folders in Windows. Then we discuss operations that you can do with files. From there, we move on to operations you can do with folders.

File Management

A *computer file* is a resource for storing information that is available to a computer program and is usually based on a form of durable storage. A file is "durable" in the sense that it remains available for other programs to use after the program that created it has finished working. Computer files are the modern counterpart of paper documents, which were traditionally kept in office and library files. A *file* or *document* is basically a blank sheet of paper that you can use to create any type of content you desire. For example, you can create a to-do list, a letter, or a set of instructions. Some of the more common file types are documents, images, videos, audio files, PDF files, Zip files, and text files. Each type of file has its own suffix. This suffix tells a program how to read and interpret the data in the file. For example, Microsoft Word documents end in .docx. Images usually end in .jpg or .png, audios in .mp3, videos in .mov or .mp4, and PDFs in .pdf. (See table 1.)

Type of File	Format
Word Document	.docx
PowerPoint Presentation	.pptx
Excel Document	.xlsx
Images	.png, .jpg, .jpeg, .tiff, .svg, .webp
Portable Document File	.pdf
Text Document	.txt
Zip File	.zip
Video	.mov, .mp4
Audio	.mp3
Executable	.exe (Windows), .dmg (Mac), .pkg (Mac).

Table 1: File types and their associated formats

A *folder* is a digital container that stores a collection of files. Folders also can contain other folders. Folders are sometimes referred to as *directories.*

The term *file management* refers to the manipulation of documents and data in files on a computer. Specifically, you can *create* a new file or *edit* an existing file and *save* it, *open* or load a pre-existing file into memory, or *close* a file without saving it. Additionally, you can group related files in *directories*. These tasks are accomplished in different ways in different operating systems and depend on the user interface design and, to some extent, the storage medium being used.

How do you manage files? In windows, you use the File Explorer. To access it, click on the yellow icon that looks like a file folder . It is on the taskbar at the bottom of your desktop. On the Macintosh, use the Finder. The access a file in Finder, click on the icon.

Through the File Explorer or Finder, you can see all the files and folders on your hard drive. You can do the following:

- Create files
- Edit, save, and print files
- Open files
- Move files
- Rename files
- Delete files
- Create folders
- Move folders
- Rename folders
- Delete folders
- Sort files and folders (e.g., by date created, last saved, title, or type of file)

> **Tip**: you may need to "enable" the details view to see the details of the files and folders (i.e., date created, last saved, title, type of file). You can do this by going to "View" and then "Details" on the File Explorer menu bar.

When you first open the File Explorer, on the left menu, you have "Quick Access," "OneDrive," "This PC," and "Network." These are like your filing cabinets. They are the main containers for storing documents and folders. In a filing cabinet, you store files (folders) in a drawer. On the computer, you store files (documents) and folders (containers that hold files and other folders) in a folder called "Documents." "Quick Access" is the place where you can "pin" or keep at the top of the access menu the most frequently used folders, so you can access them more quickly in the future. Typical folders that are pinned to Quick Access are the "Desktop," "Documents," "Downloads," "Music," "Pictures," and "Videos." The main places that you will interact with are "Documents" and "Downloads," and within that, mostly "Documents." OneDrive is Microsoft's cloud, which we will discuss when we get to Chapter 7. "This PC" is the location of your hard drive for your computer. Typically, it is named the "C" drive. Beneath these options are local drives. These are names of additional hard drives or peripherals you have connected to your computer (e.g., a USB drive). For example, if you have two hard disks in your computer, or if you have an external hard drive connected to your computer, they will show up here. Typically, you have only one hard drive.

Under "This PC," you also have a place for 3D objects. These are created with Microsoft's 3D creator program.

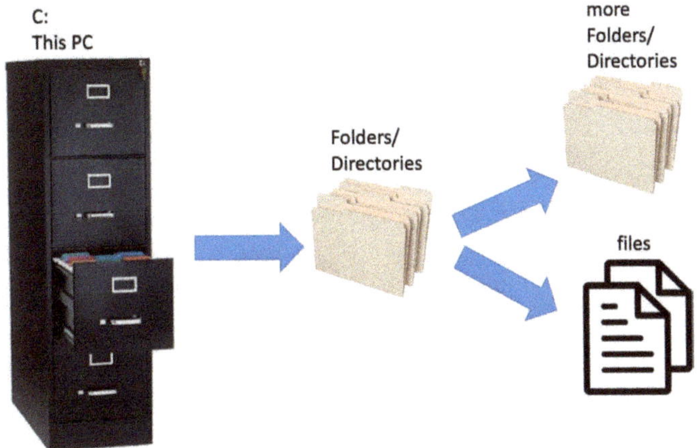

Figure 7: Files and folders and the filing cabinet analogy

File Operations

Create files

To create a new file, you will use a text editor. A discussion of how to obtain Microsoft Word and Microsoft products is beyond the scope of this book. However, you can use a free text editor that comes with Windows, called WordPad. Type "WordPad" in the search box on the taskbar. It should be the first item that comes up in the search list. Left click on it twice to open it. Once it's open, you will see a blank white "sheet" of paper. Now you can put content into the file or edit the file.

Edit, Save, and Print Files

To edit a file, place your cursor in the upper-left corner of the blank document, left click until the cursor is blinking, and start typing. When you are finished entering content onto the page, you will want to *save* the document. To do so, go to the File menu in the upper-left-hand corner and select "Save." In the popup box that appears, you will need to navigate to the proper location on your computer to save the file. Essentially, you need to tell the computer where in your filing cabinet you want to store the file, so you can retrieve it later. (See Figure 8.)

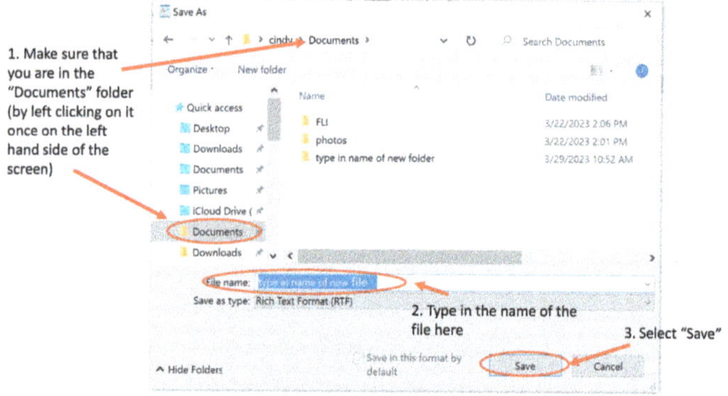

Figure 8: Saving a file

Open Files

To open a file, double left click on the file in the File Explorer.

Move Files

To move a file, drag and drop the file from where it is to where you want it to be. (See Figures 9 and 10.)

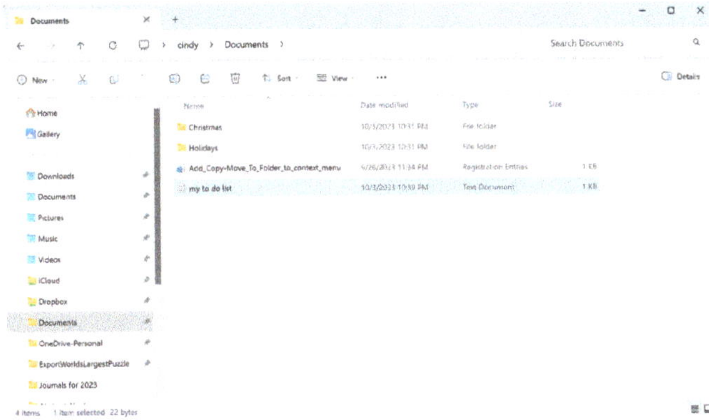

Figure 9: Step one of the "drag and drop" process to move a file to another location. Select the file by left clicking it.

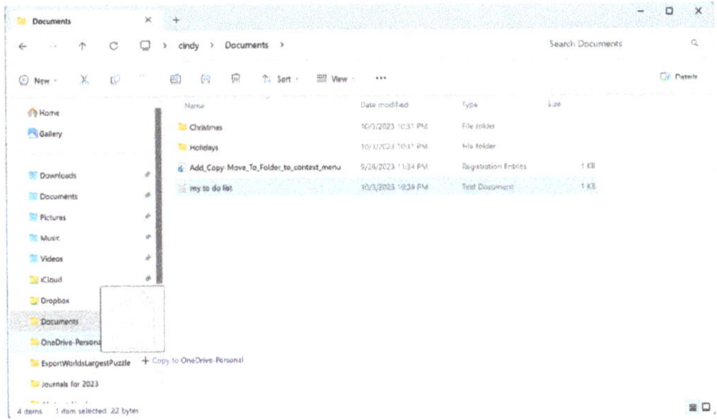

Figure 10: Step two of the drag-and-drop process to move a file to another location. After hovering a file over the desired location, release your right hand index finger from the trackpad or mouse.

Rename Files

To rename a file, left click on the name of the file to select it. (It will highlight in a blue background). Next, left click on the name of the file. The name will become surrounded by a black outline, and the filename itself will be highlighted in blue. (See Figure 12.) Now you can type a new name. Click the "Enter" key to finalize the changes.

Delete Files

To delete a file, left click on the file once to select it. When a file is selected, the background of the name turns blue. Then click the "delete" button on your keyboard. Alternatively, you can delete the file by clicking on the trashcan icon on the toolbar at the top of the File Explorer Window.

Folder Operations

Create Folders

To create a folder in Windows 11, select the New button in the upper left hand corner of the File Explorer window. Then select "Folder" from the menu.

Move Folders

To move a folder, drag and drop it from its current location to the new location.

Rename Folders

Renaming folders is similar to renaming files. To rename a folder, left click on the name of the folder to select it. It will turn the background blue. Next, left click on the name of the folder. The name will be surrounded by a black outline, and the name will be highlighted in blue.

(See Figure 11.) Now you can rename the folder. Press the "Enter" key to finalize the changes.

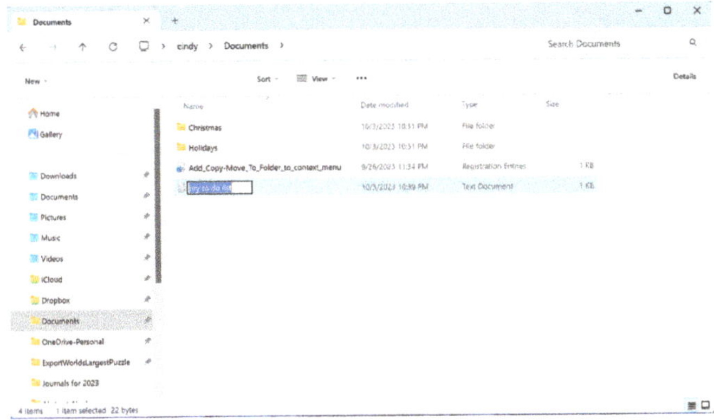

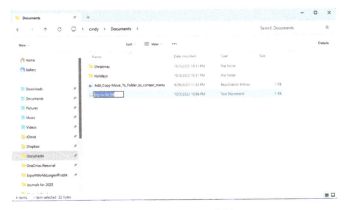

Figure 11: Renaming a folder

Delete Folders

To delete a file, left click on the file to select it. This will highlight the name of the file with a blue background. Then click the "Delete" button on your keyboard. Alternatively, you can delete the folder by clicking on the trashcan icon on the toolbar at the top of the File Explorer Window.

Sorting Files and Folders

You can sort files by clicking on the heading "Name," "Date Modified," "Type," or "Size" at the top of the File Explorer window. It will sort the files in ascending or descending order, depending on how many times you click on the header (once for ascending and twice for descending). I typically sort either by name or date modified, so I can find the files easier.

Search

Over time, you will end up with hundreds or thousands of files on your computer. Once you have files and folders set up, you may need to find a particular file on your hard disk, or you may need to find a particular file with a particular word in it. You can search for files in the File Explorer or in the desktop search tools.

Search in the File Explorer or Finder

Searching in the File Explorer or Finder searches within a user's computer files as opposed to searching the Internet. These tools are designed to find information on the user's hard disk, including email archives, text documents, audio files, images, and videos. Searches can be done on the names of files or directories, or the search can look at the specific content inside a document.

Search Using the Windows Search Bar

One of the main advantages of desktop search programs is that search results arrive within a few seconds or less. The Microsoft Windows search bar can be of some help, but it searches through Windows files and folders on your hard disk, applications on your hard disk, or information on the Internet. Note: it does not search through emails. You will have to use an email client to search through emails. Spotlight search is the equivalent search function on a Macintosh. The search bar is located on the bottom of the task bar on the desktop.

~

Exercises

Exercise 1:

FILES

You want to create a personal journal.

Create file:

Create a WordPad file with a "journal entry" in it.

Save file:

Save the file in your Documents folder with the name of "journal."

Rename file:

Rename the file to "Journal 2024."

Delete file:

You don't want anyone to accidentally read your journal, so delete "Journal 2024."

When you deleted your file, where did it go? (See Chapter 13: Oops, I Deleted My File. Now What?)

Exercise 2:

FILES

Create file:

Create a WordPad file with a to-do list in it.

Save file:

Save the file in your Documents folder with the name "my to-do list."

Rename file:

Rename the file to "my to-do list 2024."

Create file:

Create a WordPad file with a grocery list in it.

Save file:

Save the file in your Documents folder with the name of "grocery list"

Rename file:

Rename the file to "grocery list – March."

Delete file:

Delete the file "grocery list – March."

Restore file:

Restore your file from the Recycle Bin. (See Chapter 13.)

Sort files:

Sort your files in reverse alphabetical order.

Sort your files by type. (You may have to use the "detail view" to see the "type" column in the File Explorer.)

Exercise 3:

FOLDERS

Create a folder:

Create a folder in your Documents folder called "taxes." Inside "taxes," create a folder called "2023." Create another folder called "2024" and another one called "2025."

Rename folder:

Rename the "taxes" folder so that it begins with a capital letter.

Sort folders:

Sort your folders in reverse alphabetical order.

Sort your folders by date modified. (You may have to use the "detail view" to see the "date modified" column in the File Explorer.)

Exercise 4:

FOLDERS

Create a folder:

Create a folder called "Want to Learn." Inside this folder, create a folder for each subject that you are interested in learning about. Create at least three folders. Use all lowercase letters for folder names.

Rename folder:

Rename your folders so that they all begin with a capital letter.

Delete folder:

Delete one of your folders

When you deleted a folder, where did it go?

Restore your folder from the Recycle Bin. (See Chapter 13.)

Sort folders:

Sort your folders in reverse alphabetical order.

Sort your folders by date modified. (You may have to use the "detail view" to see the "date modified" column in the File Explorer.)

Chapter 5: What Do You Do with a Computer? (Using Applications)

This chapter discusses useful applications for your computer. We begin with a discussion of types of software. Next, we discuss typical applications. Finally, we conclude with how to acquire an application.

Types of Software

Free Software

Free software, also known as *freeware*, is software that is free to use. One caveat to using free software is that the software creators will most likely spam you with ads. This is how they make their money. They get paid for every ad that you click on and follow to the corresponding Internet product page. They may even get bonuses when you purchase software from an ad shown. Often you can pay a fee to have the ads removed from the app. An example of a free software application is Microsoft Games. You can play the games for free, but you will get ads every so often. You must pay to play them ad free.

Open-Source Software

Open-source software (OSS) is software in which the *source code* is made available to the public and licensed with an open-source license. This gives users the right to modify and distribute the software according to the terms of the license. Open-source software is often developed in a public, collaborative manner. Two examples of open-source software are OpenOffice and LibreOffice. You can use them as an alternative to Microsoft's 365 suite.

Closed-Source Software

Closed-source software (a.k.a. *proprietary software*) is software in which the source code is kept closed or unavailable to the public. Examples of proprietary software include Microsoft Office 365 and Adobe Photoshop.

Types of Applications

Different applications are used for different purposes. The most basic application is one that stores, retrieves, and manipulates data. Basic applications are often bundled into suites. Additional types of applications include:

- Games
- Digital photo albums
- Online collaboration applications
- Online file-sharing and storage applications
- Online meeting applications
- Note-taking applications

Office Suites

An office suite, sometimes called a productivity suite, is a collection of productivity programs that help you do work quickly and easily. The components generally are distributed together, have a consistent user interface, and can interact with one another. Microsoft 365, WordPerfect Office, OpenOffice, and LibreOffice are examples of office suites.

Existing office suites contain a wide range of components. Typically, the base components include:

- Word processor
- Spreadsheet processing
- Presentation program

Less common components of office suites include:

- Database
- Graphics
- Desktop publishing software
- Diagramming software
- Email client
- Note-taking programs
- Project-management software

Word Processing

One of the main functions that you will want to do with your computer is create files. You can use a **word processor**, also known as a **text editor**, to create files. Word processing was one of the earliest applications created for personal computers.

Word processors are descended from early text-formatting tools (sometimes called "text-justification tools" due to their only real capability). Although early word processors used tag-based markup for document formatting, most modern word processors take advantage of a graphical user interface providing some form of "what you see is what you get" ("WYSIWYG") editing. Most are powerful systems consisting of one or more programs that can produce any combination of images, graphics, and text.

Many word processors are available for all personal computer platforms. The most widely used is Microsoft Word, which is available for PC and Apple platforms.

Tip: Word processors come with templates. These include calendars, to-do lists, flyers, letters, and resumes. Feel free to use any of them.

Spreadsheet Processing

A *spreadsheet* is an interactive computer application for organization, calculations, and analysis of data in a tabular form. Spreadsheets developed as computerized simulations of paper accounting worksheets. Spreadsheet programs operate on data represented as cells in an array, organized in rows and columns. Each cell is an element that can contain either numeric or text data or the results of formulas that automatically calculate and display a value based on the contents of other cells. (See Figure 12.)

D5 *fx*

	A	B	C
1		1	
2		3	
3		9	
4		18	
5		29	
6	**Total**	**60**	
7			
8			

Figure 12: A simple spreadsheet

The user of the spreadsheet can make changes in any stored value and observe the effects on calculated values. This makes the spreadsheet useful for "what-if" analysis since many cases can be rapidly investigated without tedious manual recalculation. Modern spreadsheet software can have multiple interacting sheets and can display data either as text and numerals or in graphical form.

In addition to the fundamental operations of arithmetic and mathematical functions, spreadsheets have built-in functions for common financial and statistical operations. Such calculations as net present value or standard deviation can be applied to tabular data with a pre-programmed function in a formula. Spreadsheet programs also provide conditional expressions, functions to convert between text and numbers, and functions that operate on strings of text.

Spreadsheets have replaced paper-based systems throughout the business world. Although they were first developed for accounting or bookkeeping tasks, they now are used extensively in any context where tabular lists are built, sorted, and shared.

Databases

A *database* is an organized collection of data. Formally, "database" refers to the data themselves along with their supporting data structures. Databases are created to operate on large quantities of information by creating easy-to-use interfaces that allow for inputting, storing, retrieving, and manipulating that information.

Database management systems (DBMSs) are software applications designed to interact with the user, other applications, and the database itself to capture and analyze data. A general-purpose DBMS is a software system designed to allow for the definition, creation, querying, update, and administration of databases. Well-known DBMSs include MySQL, Microsoft SQL Server, Oracle, dBASE, FoxPro, IBM DB2, and FileMaker Pro. A database is not generally portable across different DBMSs, but different DBMSs can interoperate by using standards such as SQL and ODBC to allow a single application to work with more than one database.

Because they are so closely related, the term "database" when used casually often refers to both a DBMS and the data it manipulates.

Presentation Processing

Presentations consist of a number of individual pages or *slides*. The "slide" analogy is a reference to the projector. A better analogy would be the "foils" (or transparencies/ plastic sheets) that are shown using an overhead projector, although they are in decline now. Slides can contain text, graphics, sound, movies, and other objects that may be arranged freely. The presentation can be printed, displayed live on a computer, or navigated through by a presenter. For larger audiences the computer display is often projected using a video projector. Slides can also form the basis of webcasts.

PowerPoint is the slide-based presentation program developed by Microsoft. It was officially launched on May 22, 1990, as a part of the Microsoft Office suite.

Games

Games have been around since the dawn of computers, and they are a fun way to pass the time. Games can be played on your PC or collaboratively online.

On Your PC

Some games come preloaded on your computer. These include games such as solitaire, Minesweeper, and Hearts. Games can also be purchased in stores or online. If you're a new computer user, I recommend that you find a game that interests you and play it so that you can get a feel for your keyboard. More importantly, it will help you get past their fear of "accidentally doing something that will mess up the computer."

Some suppliers of free and purchasable games can be found on Steam (https://store.steampowered.com/), Popcap.com, Gamehouse.com, and Bigfishgames.com. Other games can also be downloaded from the app store that comes preloaded on your computer.

Collaboratively Online

Massively multiplayer online games (MMOG)

Massively multiplayer online games were made possible with the growth of broadband Internet access in many developed countries, using the Internet to allow hundreds of thousands of players to play the same game together at the same time. Many different styles of massively multiplayer games are available, such as:

- MMORPG (massively multiplayer online role-playing game): examples include *Dragon Warriors* and *Dungeon World.*
- MMORTS (massively multiplayer online real-time strategy): examples include *Warcraft* and *Age of Mythology.*
- MMOFPS (massively multiplayer online first-person shooter): examples include *Battlefield* and *Quake.*
- MMOSG (massively multiplayer online social game): Facebook has a lot of online social games.

Of course, there are educational games as well, such as *Oregon Trail* and *Where in the World is Carmen Sandiego?*

Boatloadpuzzles.com offers crossword puzzles playable online or on paper. You can also go to Dictionary.com and take advantage of their word games. Another source for a word game is Worddynamo.com. In addition to being fun, these word puzzles also exercise your mind. I make it a matter of routine to play three daily crossword sites each morning to awaken my mind.

Digital Photo Albums

If you are into photography, a plethora of applications are available to help you manage your photos, apply special effects to your photos, and publish them.

Digital cameras were made to supply the need for more precise pictures and also to permit you to download them onto your computer. But don't let that box of "real" pictures get you down. If you have a multi-purpose printer (printer, fax, copier, and scanner in a single all-in-one printer), you can scan those pictures and save them to your hard drive, the cloud, or an external drive for safe storage.

Websites such as Download.cnet.com provide access to a number of free photo software applications as well as other types of applications. Photo editing apps can also be found in the app store. Additionally, Adobe has a suite of photo editing apps, including Photoshop and Elements.

Online Collaboration

A tool that is useful for online collaboration is Google Docs. Google Docs is a suite of document tools that you can access online from anywhere in the world. You also can easily share and collaborate with other people in real time synchronously or asynchronously.

Google Docs, Sheets, and Slides are productivity apps that let you create different kinds of online documents, work on them in real time with other people, and store them on Google Drive.

Google Docs

Google Docs is an online word processor that lets you create and format text documents and collaborate with other people in real time. Here's what you can do with Google Docs.

- Upload a Word document and convert it to a Google document
- Add flair and formatting to your documents by adjusting margins, spacing, fonts, and colors
- Invite other people to collaborate on a document, giving them edit, comment, or view access
- Collaborate online in real time and chat with other collaborators while inside the document
- View your document's revision history and roll back to any previous version
- Download a Google document to your desktop as a Word, OpenOffice, RTF, PDF, HTML, or zip file
- Translate a document to a different language
- Email your documents to other people as attachments

To learn more about Google Docs, check out the Google Docs getting started guide.

Google Sheets

Google Sheets is an online spreadsheet app that lets you create and format spreadsheets and simultaneously work with other people. Here's what you can do with Google Sheets.

- Import and convert Excel, .csv, .txt, and .ods documents to a Google spreadsheet

- Export to Excel, .csv, .txt, .ods, PDF, and HTML formats
- Use formula editing to perform calculations on your data, and use formatting make it look the way you'd like
- Chat in real time with others who are editing your spreadsheet
- Create charts with your data
- Embed a spreadsheet—or individual sheets of your spreadsheet—on your blog or website

For more information about Google Sheets, check out the Google Sheets getting started guide.

Google Slides

Google Slides is an online presentation app similar to PowerPoint that allows you to show off your work in a visual way. Here's what you can do with Google Slides.

- Create and edit presentations
- Edit a presentation with friends or coworkers and share it with others
- Import .pptx and .pps files and convert them to Google presentations
- Download your presentations as a PDF, PPT, or .txt file
- Insert images and videos into your presentation
- Publish and embed your presentations on a website

For more information about Google Slides, check out the Google Slides getting started guide

Online File Sharing and Storage

Sometimes, you need to store files in the cloud and share them with other people. For example, emails generally only allow you to attach files that are less than 23 MB in size. If you want to share a 50 MB video, you will have to use a file storage/sharing application. To do this, upload your file to this cloud, and then you will receive a link that you can share with others. Then put the link into your email, and people will be able click on the link to download your files. You can share folders this way as well. Two good applications to use are Dropbox (www.dropbox.com) and Box (www.box.com). You also can download desktop and mobile clients for each of these.

Online Meeting Tools

These tools let you do video or audio conferences with other people. Three common online meeting tools are Zoom, Skype, and Google Meet.

Note-Taking Apps

Another tool you might find interesting are note-taking apps. Three common note-taking apps are Evernote, Notion, and OneNote.

How to Get an Application on Your Computer

There are two main ways that you can get an app. You can download it from the app store, or you can download it from the Internet.

In the App Store

The app store is the virtual space where applications are viewed, searched for, and purchased. It is akin to a bookstore, but instead of books, it contains software applications. You can search through the store, or you can look at recommendations from the store. The software in the store has been vetted by Microsoft (Windows), google (google Play) or Apple (mac) to make sure that it won't harm your computer.

Common categories of apps include

- Productivity
- Games
- Social networking
- Books
- Business
- Dining

On the Web

The second way to acquire software applications is to download them from the Internet. One caution about this is that you never know what people are slipping into the application, such as viruses and trojan horses. (We'll have a more in-depth discussion in Chapter 9: Security.) One example of an application that you should download is Adobe Acrobat Reader. This application allows you to view PDF files.

> **Key takeaway**: For anything you can think of, there is probably an app for it! Take plenty of time to explore the app store.

Note: To *uninstall* a program on your computer, go to "Settings," click on "Apps" and then "Installed apps." Locate the application that you want to uninstall. On the right-hand side of the app, there are three horizontal dots. Click on them, and then click on "uninstall."

~

Exercises

Exercise 1:

Open a new Google doc. (Hint: go to docs.google.com, and start a new blank document.) Write a *short* ghost story. Invite a friend to collaborate on the story with you. (Hint: go to "Share" in the upper right-hand corner, and enter their email address in the input box.) Have your friend edit your story. View the changes.

Exercise 2:

You are going on vacation with your best friend. For your dream vacation, you will need to create a shared budget. Open a new Google sheet. (Hint: go to sheets.google.com, and start a new blank sheet.) Create a budget. Invite your best friend to edit the budget. (Hint: go to "Share" in the upper right-hand corner, and enter their email address in the input box.) Have your friend edit your budget. View the changes.

Exercise 3:
Create a slideshow about your most recent vacation in Google Slides or another presentation editor of your choice.

Exercise 4:
Create a slide "album" filled with pictures of you and your best friend. Find pictures of you and your best friend. Open a new Google presentation (Hint: go to slides.google.com and start a new blank presentation.) Create slides of your pictures of you and your friend. Put some text below each picture, indicating the place and date that the picture was taken and any notes you want to add about the photograph. Invite your best friend to edit the album. (Hint: go to "Share" in the upper right-hand corner, and enter their email address in the input box.) Have your friend edit your presentation. View the changes.

Apps

Exercise 1:
Search for a program in the app store called "Microsoft Sticky Notes." It's free. Download and install Sticky Notes on your computer.

Exercise 2:
Search for and download a productivity application from the app store.

Exercise 3:
Download "Wordle" from the Microsoft app store.

Exercise 4:

Find and acquire a game. Choose from one of the following categories or choose your own category: strategy, car, shooting, action, puzzle.

> **Note**: To install a program on your computer from the app store, click on "get" from the Microsoft store. When it's finished downloading, click "install," and click "Yes" on the subsequent popup that asks if you want to allow this program to modify your computer.

Exercise 5:

Download Adobe Acrobat Reader from the Internet. Adobe reader can be found at the following URL: https://get.adobe.com/reader/.

> **Note**: To download a file from the Internet, you will need an installer file. An installer file usually ends with a .exe for windows computers and .pkg or .dmg for a Macintosh. Double click it, then follow the on-screen prompts.

> **Security Tip**: Be cautious when downloading software. Many viruses are lurking on the Internet, so you should only download and install applications from a safe and trusted source.

Exercise 6:

Go to Zoom.us, and create a free account. Login. Create a meeting, then invite a friend to the meeting. At the allocated time, start the meeting and then have a short online discussion. Look at the bottom of the Zoom window for a "Share screen" button. Share your screen with your friend. End the meeting.

Chapter 6: The Internet

In this chapter, we discuss the Internet. We begin with basic concepts about the Internet and how to connect to it. Then we discuss web browsers and some of their most common functionalities. Next, we discuss search engines. After that, we discuss common websites that you will want to know about.

Ode to the Internet

the Internet,
Oh how I love it
for it is:
a shopping mall
an accountant
a radio
a television
a game room
a library
a school
a church

a club
a magazine
a phone book
a directory
a teleconference
a social gathering
a dictionary
a thesaurus
a think tank
a calculator
a calendar
a newspaper
a game
a laboratory
a museum
a network
a publisher
a periodical
an advertisement
a broker
a tutor
a cheat sheet
a spy
a computer program
a microcosm of society
a question you never knew you had
a ubiquitous virtual reality at your fingertips every hour of the day; every day of the year
where all you have to do is imagine an idea, a thought, a desire, a question

and you can find it itself, find a where it lies, learn about it,
and even how to create it
it is, in effect, an extension of your very imagination!
and, best of all, it's free!*

*Well sort of. If you're not on public Wi-Fi, you probably have to pay an Internet service provider to get your Internet services.

I wrote this poem in 2003. Since that time, many more functions have been added. The main takeaway is that you can do/find almost anything on the Internet.

What Is the Internet?

The Internet is a global system of interconnected computer networks that use the standard Internet protocol suite (TCP/IP) to serve several billions of users worldwide. It is a *network of networks* that consists of millions of private, public, academic, business, and government networks, from local to global scope, that are linked by a broad array of electronic, wireless, and optical networking technologies. The Internet carries an extensive range of informational resources and services, such as the interlinked hypertext documents of the World Wide Web (WWW), the infrastructure to support email, and peer-to-peer networks.

How Do I Connect to the Internet?

Internet Service Provider

To connect to the Internet, you'll need an *Internet Service Provider (ISP).* An ISP provides services such as Internet access, Internet transit, domain name registration and hosting, dial-up access, leased line access and colocation. Internet service providers are organized in various forms, such as commercial, community-owned, non-profit, or otherwise privately owned networks. They operate using cable networks, phone lines, or satellite dishes.

Wi-Fi

Another way to connect to the Internet is to hop onto free Wi-Fi *hotspots.* Some hotspots are password protected, and some are not. Hotspots in hotels, for example, are usually password protected. You'll have to ask the front desk what the name of the network and password are. Examples of non-password-protected hotspots include turnpike rest areas or Starbucks coffee shops. Cybersecurity experts advise that you should never use public Wi-Fi, at least for important business or online banking transactions, because of what is called *man-in-the-middle attacks.* This is where hackers can position themselves between you and the hotspot, intercepting and reading your communication, and then relaying it to the destination as if nothing happened. Then the hacker steals your information. Another problem with public Wi-Fi is that it's easy for someone to slip in *malware* that gets downloaded to your computer when you connect to the hotspot. For the most part, public Wi-Fi hotspots in the

US don't have this problem, but I've heard that this can be a big problem in foreign countries. Another caveat to using public Wi-Fi is that there are often terms of agreement for use. For example, one of the most common caveats is that you are not supposed to do any illegal activities on the hotspot. The Ohio Turnpike terms of use state that "The Site may not be used in such a manner as to violate any applicable law. The Site may not be used for the purposes of destroying, disrupting or interrupting any software, hardware or any part of the Internet, including denial of service attacks, imposition of an unreasonable or disproportionately large load on our infrastructure, or virus dissemination."[1]

How Can I Access the Internet?

Once you have Internet service, you connect to the Internet by selecting the Wi-Fi icon ( ). Next, you will select a Wi-Fi network, and if required, enter the network password. Once your computer is connected to Wi-Fi, you can send and receive information over the Internet.

To access the Internet, you will need a web browser.

Web Browsers

A *web browser* is an application that connects to a server on the Internet and displays the information returned from the server onto your computer screen. It does this through the basic language of the Internet (hypertext markup language or HTML), along with some additional languages such as JavaScript. For example, when you tell

1 https://www.ohioturnpike.org/terms-of-use

the web browser to go to a site like www.google.com, that site returns HTML code to the browser, which then determines the best way to display the page, so it displays in a visually appealing way, as designed by the website creator.

There are five main web browsers.

- Firefox (owned by the Mozilla Foundation)
- Chrome (owned by Google)
- Safari (owned by Apple)
- Edge (owned by Microsoft)
- DuckDuckGo (owned by an independent company)

Edge and Safari come with your computer's operating system. You will have to download Firefox, Chrome, and DuckDuckGo. To download Firefox, go to https://www.mozilla.org/en-US/firefox/new/. Then download Chrome, go to https://www.google.com/chrome/. To download DuckDuckGo, go to https://duckduckgo.com/windows/. Firefox and DuckDuckGo are also available from the Microsoft store.

Which Browser Should I Use?

All of the browsers mentioned above have capabilities that are comparable to each other. What's different about each is the number of capabilities that the browser begins with in the user interface. Therefore, which browser to use is a matter of personal preference. Chrome begins with a minimal user interface. DuckDuckGo also begins with a small set of features in the user interface. Firefox begins with an intermediate user interface, and Edge begins with a more complex user interface. Users then can add additional features via browser plug-ins.

What Is a Browser Used For?

A browser is used to *surf* the web. Browsers also let you download files from the Internet or a cloud to your hard disk.

I Downloaded a File. Where Did It Go?

Generally, when you download a file, it goes into your "downloads" folder on your computer. This folder can be accessed through your browser or through the File Explorer. It usually appears under the main browser menu. The downloads folder is designed to be a temporary storage location. If you want to save your file permanently, you should move it out of your downloads folder onto your hard disk or into the cloud. Otherwise, it can be deleted, sometimes, unexpectedly. In fact, there are processes in every browser for "clearing the cache," "clearing your cookies," and "clearing the downloads folder." These items are temporary files generated by the browser and stored on your computer. When you "clear" any of these items, you delete all the data (files) in each corresponding location. It's good to clear this data from your browser periodically. The option to clear these is usually located under the browser's Settings menu.

About Browsers

The basic elements of a browser are:

- Address bar
- Homepage
- Reading List
- Favorites bar (also sometimes called a Bookmarks bar)

- Tabs
- Settings

See Figure 13.

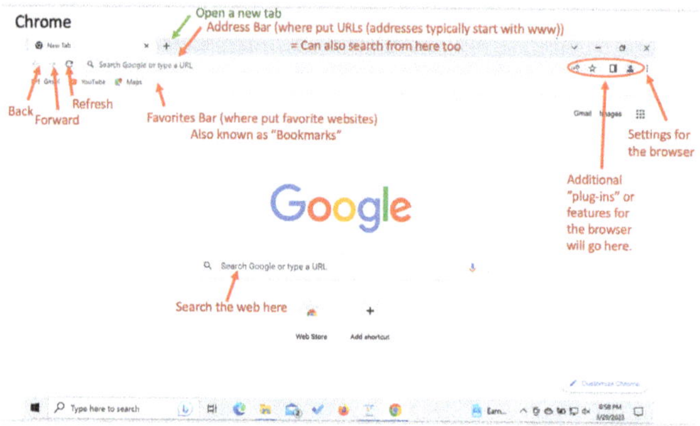

Figure 13: A web browser

Address Bar

The address bar is where you enter a *Uniform Resource Locator (URL)*, or a unique virtual address, into the browser. A URL usually starts with www, such as www.google.com. You can also put search terms in the address bar, and the browser will use a default search engine to search for those terms. I recommend against putting search terms in the address bar because people tend to get confused about if they should be entering a URL or a search term in this bar.

Homepage

This is the main page, or set of pages, that open when you first start your browser. It usually contains a search engine field, some of your most commonly visited websites, and trending news stories.

Reading List

A list of Internet articles that can be saved and read on a later date.

Favorites Bar (a.k.a. Bookmarks Bar)

The favorites bar is a special location (usually a toolbar below the main address bar) where you can store your favorite, or most frequently visited web pages, for easy retrieval in the future. When you save a web page for later retrieval and viewing, it is called "bookmarking" a website.

Tip: How to Create a Bookmark

1. Open a web browser
2. Go to a web page that you want to bookmark
3. Press the "star" button next to the address bar
   a. Give the bookmark a custom name (label). Note: this label is solely for your reference.
   b. Click the "Done" button.

> **Note**: You may have to enable the view of the bookmarks bar before you can see your favorites bar beneath the address bar. To enable the view of the bookmarks bar, go to your browser settings, then to "Bookmarks and Lists," then to "Show Bookmarks Bar."

Tabs

A "tab" is a space where you can view a web page. You can open multiple tabs at once. For example, you may want to check your email and read the news at the same time. You can switch between tabs by clicking on the tab name at the top of the browser screen. To open a new tab, click the "plus" button next to the tab name. (See Figure 13.)

Settings

These are various features that can be changed or personalized within the browser. Some common settings are:

- Show favorites (bookmarks) bar
- Set homepage(s)
- See or clear "History" (past web pages that you have visited)
- Clearing cookies
- Viewing stored passwords

I encourage you to explore additional browser settings.

Searching (Surfing) the Net

If you know what site you want to go to, you can type its URL in the address bar and go to it. If you don't know what site you want to go to, or if you want to search for something on the web, you will have to use a *search engine.* A search engine is an application that is aware of all the websites on the Internet. It scans the Internet, searches through the content of each web page, and returns the top result of your search to you in a convenient format. There are four main search engines—Google, DuckDuckGo, Yahoo!, and Bing.

Google

Google is owned by Google Inc. One note about using Google is that it saves all of your searches. Then it uses that information to advertise to you and to store the latest trending searches on the web. One thing you can do to minimize your stored search history is to configure it in your Google account settings. The Google search engine is located at www.google.com.

DuckDuckGo

DuckDuckGo is a search engine that has more privacy than Google, Yahoo, and Bing. It does not record your search history or any other information that can tie you to a search in its search engine. It has a search engine and a web browser. The DuckDuckGo search engine is located at www.duckduckgo.com.

Yahoo!

Yahoo is a search engine owned by Yahoo! Inc. It is located at www.yahoo.com.

Bing

Bing is Microsoft's search engine. It is the default search engine in Edge and on Windows computers. The Bing search engine is located at www.bing.com.

Note: Your browser will let you store passwords that you use to log in to common websites. You can decide whether or not you want to let the browser store passwords for you. Generally, it is safe to do so.

Security Tip: If you let the browser store your passwords, use a strong password for your browser profile, and turn on *two-factor authentication* for your browser. Then if someone hacks into your browser profile, they won't be able to get login access to every password and website you log in to, including banking websites.

Note: Be careful not to confuse the web browser with the search engine. Recall, a *web browser* lets you go to a particular web address and see what's there. A *search engine* lets you search through all of the web pages on the Internet. Using a web browser is like going to a unique physical address and looking at the house that's on the lot. A search engine is like looking through the yellow pages/ phone book and searching for a phone number or other piece of information.

Internet Domains

Internet sites are grouped by "domain." Most websites are commercial; therefore, they have the *.com* suffix. Non-profit sites usually will have a *.org* domain, and educational websites will end in *.edu,* Foreign websites usually have the two character abbreviation for the country (i.e., Canadian websites end with *.ca* and German websites in *.de*). There are also *.net* domains and more recently, additional domains have been added, such as *.io* and *.tv*.

Uniform Resource Locators (URLs)

A URL is an address for a web page. Each URL is unique and uniquely identifies a web page or other content that is distributed to you (the client) by a server on the back end. An example of a URL is http://www.google.com. Here, *http* represents the protocol being used to transmit data between the server on which the web page is located and you. The two most common protocols are http and https. A domain usually begins with *www*, which stands for "world wide web." www is a subdomain, or a separate virtual space, under your domain name. Note: www can often be left off of the address when entering a URL into the web browser address bar (i.e., you can enter "google. com" instead of "www.google.com."). Next comes the domain name itself. This is the actual unique address of the website. (e.g., google). Finally, you have the suffix or top-level domain. Extra data can be tacked on to the end of the URL. These are special parameters that are used in website applications while processing data between your computer and the server on which the application is located. A good analogy for a URL is your house. Your unique mailing address is analogous to a domain name. A particular location within your house (e.g., the garage, the living room) is analogous to a subdomain. The suffix is analogous to what type of house you have (e.g., apartment, duplex, townhouse).

Common Websites

Below are some of the commonly accessed websites that you might be interested in. This is not a comprehensive list. It is intended as a basic starter pack of common websites that you'll want to know about. Website names are not case sensitive, so don't worry about capitalization. I capitalized some for readability purposes.

Social Media

- Facebook.com
- Twitter.com
- Instagram.com
- Pinterest.com
- Flickr.com
- TikTok.com

Search Engines

- Google.com
- DuckDuckGo.com
- Yahoo.com
- Bing.com

Streaming Video

- YouTube.com
- Vimeo.com
- Twitch.tv

Informational

- Wikipedia.org
- Dictionary.com (also provides a daily crossword)
- Weather.com
- Yellowpages.com or YP.com
- Reddit.com
- Ted.com

Streaming/TV

- Netflix.com
- Hulu.com
- Amazon.com/gp/video/storefront (Amazon Prime Video)
- Rottentomatoes.com

Directions

- Mapquest.com
- Maps.google.com

Email

- Gmail.com
- Yahoo.com
- AOL.com

Shopping

- Amazon.com
- Paypal.com
- Ebay.com
- Etsy.com

Miscellaneous

- Craigslist.org
- Angi.com

Bookstores

- Amazon.com
- Barnesandnoble.com

Cloud/File Storage

- Dropbox.com
- iCloud.com
- OneDrive.com

Video Calls

- Zoom.us
- Skype.com
- Meet.google.com

Dating

- Match.com
- Eharmony.com
- catholicsingles.com
- christianmingle.com

Educational Institutions

- ND.edu
- Mit.edu
- Unm.edu

Educational Sites

- Lynda.com
- Your Local Library (note: you will have to look up their web address)
- Udemy.com
- Udacity.com
- Ed2go.com

Languages

- Translate.google.com

Sports

- NFL.com
- ESPN.com
- Cbssports.com

Non-profit organizations

- volunteermatch.org

Travel

- Expedia.com
- Travelocity.com
- Trivago.com
- AirBnB.com*

Design

- Canva.com

Website Creation

- Wordpress.com

Cabs

- Uber.com*

Services that drop off food at house

- Ubereats.com*
- Grubhub.com*

*Each of these websites have an accompanying mobile application as well.

Online Shopping

Sometimes, you will want to use the Internet to do online shopping. Certain websites dedicated to shopping. Some examples include amazon.com and ebay.com. In addition to these websites, you can also go to google.com, type in the item that you are searching for and then press the "Shopping" subcategory (beneath the search bar after you search for an item). Additionally, you can go to shopping.google.com to go directly to Google's shopping marketplace. Here you can filter by price, type of shop owner, condition, seller, and more. To make a purchase online, you need to use a credit card, PayPal, or a similar service, such as Klarna. See Chapter 8: Online Banking and the HTTPS Protocol.

Music and Radio

Most music these days can be purchased through the cloud from iTunes or Xbox. When you purchase a song through one of these sites, it is available on any computer that you sign into your account from.

Radio is also available. iTunes has a radio service built into it. You can also listen to radio stations directly from the Internet. There are pages that contain thousands of radio stations (e.g., live365.com, tunein.com, and iheart.com), and there are specific radio station pages, which can be found by going directly to the radio station website (e.g., go to wfrn.com, and click on the "listen live" link). Additional places you can go to listen to music include pandora.com, spotify.com, and music.youtube.com. Many music sites also have the ability to play *podcasts* in addition to music. A podcast is an audio recording that can range from several minutes to several hours. Podcasts typically feature interviews with speakers, debates, or speakers talking about a particular subject.

TV/Online Streaming

In addition to music, you can *stream* or play television shows and movies over the Internet. The server breaks a movie or TV show into bite-size chunks (called packets) and sends (streams) it over the Internet packet by packet to your computer, tablet, or smartphone. The video is stored in the cloud, but the packets are buffered on your computer (saved in small bite-size chunks). Some streaming services give you the option to download an entire movie or TV show. You usually have to pay a subscription fee per month for streaming services. Example free streaming services are Roku, Tubi, and Pluto. Example paid streaming services include Netflix, Hulu, Peacock, and Amazon Prime TV.

> **Note:** If you are interested in movie and TV show reviews, visit www.rottentomatoes.com.

Calendars

Google has a suite of tools that enable online calendar collaboration and organization. One tool is called Google Calendar, and it's stored in the Google cloud. This way, all you need is access to any computer, and you can log into Google and see your calendar. This is very useful for online collaboration.

Directions

What if you need to get somewhere, but you don't know how to get there or how long it will take? In this case, you can use online direction websites. Two common direction websites are MapQuest and Google Maps. Not only do these sites give you directions, but they also provide alternate routes, and they show which routes are congested with traffic or construction. You can view the directions/confirm the route online and then print out the directions. Another neat feature is that you can send directions to your phone or tablet. A second cool feature is that some map programs will show you the location of speed cameras, police officers trying to catch speeders, and red-light cameras along your route.

One final note about the Internet: For anything you can think of, there is probably an application for it. Don't be afraid to open a web browser. Go to www.google.com, and search for it!

~

Exercises

Exercise 1:

If desired, download Firefox, Chrome, or DuckDuckGo. To download Firefox, go to https://www.mozilla.org/en-US/firefox/new/. To download Chrome, go to https://www.google.com/chrome/. To download DuckDuckGo, go to https://duckduckgo.com/windows/.

Exercise 2:

- View passwords stored in your browser. (Hint: Go to your browser's settings.)
- Clear the cache in your browser. (Hint: Go to your browser's settings.)
- Go to www.google.com and bookmark it (i.e., put it on your favorites bar).
- Open a new tab.
  a. Search for "how to tie dye a shirt."
  b. Open another tab.
    i. search for "How big is the state of Indiana?"
- Open a new tab.
  a. Open your email.

        i. Check your email.
    b. Open another tab.
        i. Go to abcnews.com, and read a news article.
    c. Go back to your email tab.
        i. Check your email again.

Exercise 3:

In your favorite web browser:

- Bookmark Wikipedia.org (i.e., put it on your favorites bar).
- Bookmark your email (e.g., gmail.com or att.net).
- Go to your settings, and look at the history of web pages that you have visited.
- Go to google.com, and do the following searches:

1. who were Lewis and Clark
2. how many inches are in a yard
3. how do I cook cornbread
4. how do I create a desktop shortcut in windows 10/11
5. How do I set the "wallpaper" in Chromebook
6. How do I set the "wallpaper" in windows 10/11
7. Ask Google anything you would like!

Exercise 4:

Explore three websites listed in the section on Common Websites.

Exercise 5:

Find your local library website

Exercise 6:

Choose three of the following activities.

- Find the same size/make of shoe at two local retail outlets by searching online. Compare prices.
- Look up a friend's phone number online using their street address, *or* find a friend's street address using their telephone number. (Hint: type their information into Google.)
- Find online instructions to create a desktop shortcut for your operating system.
- Look up a "top ten" product list for a kitchen appliance or power tool.
- Find a local outlet for the product "Wyler's Italian Ices."
- Find TIL (Today I Learned) on Reddit.com. Now find a "dad" joke.
- Check a news story at Snope.com.
- Troubleshoot a computer problem online by using the Google search engine.
- Make a file containing Microsoft "hot keys" for Word by copying an online page into a Word document.
- Capture a map of Indiana from Wikipedia, and paste it into a Word document.
- Print a web page (Go to File → Print, or press Ctrl + P).
- Find a product review.
- Find your local newspaper online.
- Find an eagle cam.
- Find out how to change a tire on YouTube.
- Find a product on Amazon (a book or other product).
- Order movie tickets—just go through the steps; don't place the order.

- Order plane tickets—just go through steps; don't place the order.

Chapter 7: The Cloud

In this chapter, we discuss the cloud. We begin with what a cloud is. Then we discuss different types of clouds. Next, we continue with how to access the cloud in Windows. Finally, we conclude with a discussion of whether you should store your data in the cloud or on your hard drive.

What Is the Cloud?

The cloud is not a physical object. It's a group of networked servers connected to each other that perform a particular function. Some clouds use computing power to run applications or deliver a service. Other clouds store data. The nice thing about the cloud is that you can store your data in the cloud and then access it from any device (e.g., computer, tablet, phone) at any time. The cloud syncs your data across all of your devices.

More and more services are being put into the cloud, including services that help you manage and store files and documents, pictures, books, applications, TV shows, and music. When you sign in to a cloud, you can see all the items that you purchased or stored there, including books, music, applications, and file backups.

There are many clouds. Every notable computer company has its own cloud. Common clouds include Kindle, AWS, iCloud, OneDrive, Adobe Creative Cloud, and Google Drive. Note that these clouds do not "talk" to/exchange data with one another. They are completely separate, and often they compete with one another for your business.

Monetization of the Cloud

Some clouds may give you a limited amount of storage for free, but after that, they charge a fee to get more space. For example, every Google account comes with 15 GB of cloud storage, which is shared across Google Drive, Gmail, and Google Photos. Every Yahoo account comes with 1 TB of free storage. Every Hotmail account comes with 15 GB of email storage space. Microsoft 365 subscribers get 50 GB of space. When you sign up for iCloud, you get 5 GB of free storage. OneDrive also gives you 5 GB of free storage.

Different Clouds

Amazon

One of Amazon's clouds is Kindle. Kindle is used to store digital Kindle books. When you purchase a digital book, you cannot print the book. You have to read it with a Kindle reader. You can access a Kindle reader for free on amazon's website, download a Kindle app through the app store or from Amazon's website, or you can purchase a Kindle e-reader from Amazon.

Amazon's other main cloud is AWS (Amazon Web Services). It is mostly used by commercial companies, small businesses, and web developers.

Apple

Apple's version of the cloud is called iCloud. iCloud stores files, iCloud domain emails, calendars, notes, and photos from Macintosh computers, tablets, and iPhones. iCloud syncs data across all of your Apple products. You can access iCloud through Finder on an Apple computer. You can also access the cloud on the web at iCloud.com. You can download a desktop client that will allow you to access iCloud from the File Explorer.

Microsoft

Microsoft's cloud is OneDrive. OneDrive stores files and data from various programs on Windows-based computers. You can access OneDrive from the File Explorer on a Windows computer. Look on the left-hand-side area for a blue cloud with "OneDrive" right next to it. If the arrowhead to the left of the cloud is pointing to the right, left click on it, and folders will expand beneath it. If the arrowhead is pointed down, then you will see your folders beneath it. These folders are in the cloud. Otherwise, on an Apple computer, you can download a desktop client that will allow you to access OneDrive in Finder.

Tip: There are two "Documents" folders in Windows. One Documents folder is on your hard disk. The other is in the cloud (OneDrive). Be careful not to confuse the two. You can tell if you are in the cloud Documents folder because there will be a *status* column next to the file name. In the Documents folder on your hard drive, there is no status column.

Adobe

Adobe's cloud is called Adobe Creative Cloud. Here you can store files created from all of Adobe products (e.g., Photoshop, Illustrator, InDesign). You can also access Creative Cloud online at Adobe.com.

Google

Google's cloud is called Google Drive. Google Drive stores files across Google's suite of applications (e.g., Google Docs, Google Sheets, Google Forms, Google Slides). A nice thing about Google Drive is that it's easy to share access to files with other people. This makes it easy to collaborate with others on projects or presentations. Google Drive is located at drive.google.com. You can download a Google Drive client for your desktop. This allows you to access files through the File Explorer (on Windows) or Finder (on the Mac).

How Do I Access the Cloud?

Each cloud is accessed differently. Kindle's cloud can be accessed from Amazon's amazon.com website, through the Kindle app, or from a Kindle tablet. iCloud can be accessed through an Apple computer, iPad, or iPhone. It can also be accessed online at iCloud.com or through a desktop client in File Explorer on a windows computer. OneDrive can be accessed at onedrive.com, through a Windows computer, or through a desktop client in Finder (on a Mac). Adobe Creative Cloud can be accessed through the adobe.com website or through the Adobe Creative Cloud desktop or mobile client.

Hard Drive Versus the Cloud

You can store your digital data in two main places—your hard drive and the cloud. The cloud, as you know, is a collection of servers that are running in a specific physical location. When you store a file in the cloud, it is stored on a server at that cloud location. When you store a file on your hard drive, it is stored on the physical disk located inside your computer. For example, when you take a picture on your smartphone, it is stored in iCloud or Google Photos, depending on if you use an iPhone or an Android or a Pixel phone. Photos also can be stored on your phone's internal memory. When you upload photos to Instagram or Facebook, you are uploading a copy of the photo to the Facebook or Instagram cloud.

Where Should I Store My Data?

Where you store your data depends on what you are most comfortable doing and how much you want to spend to store your data. There are three main places where you can store your data.

1. ***Hard drive***

   If you store data on your hard drive, then you don't have to pay for the cloud. However, if you accidently break your computer or lose it, you will lose your data. If you store your documents on your hard drive, be sure to back them up frequently to an external drive.

2. ***External hard drive***

   You can purchase an external hard drive at Best Buy, Office Max, Staples, or online at Amazon or other retailers. Back up your data frequently, and store your external drive in a different location than you store your computer. If something happens to that location, you will lose all of your data (e.g., your house burns down). (See Chapter 12: Backup and Recovery Concepts).

3. ***The Cloud***

   If you store your data in the cloud, you will have to pay for storage after a certain point. The good side of storing data in the cloud is that you can access it from any computer, tablet, or smartphone from anywhere in the world, and it is synchronized across all of your devices. That is, all of your devices can access the same documents, videos, songs, or photos. If you delete a file on the cloud, it will be deleted across all devices as well.

If you have a small number of files, you may consider storing them on your hard drive and then backing them up occasionally to an external drive. If you have very important files or files that you need to access from any device at any time, then you may consider storing them in the cloud.

My Cloud Account Is Full. What Should I Do?

If your cloud account is full, you can do one of three things.

1. Purchase additional space.
2. Delete old files.
3. Remove older files from the cloud, and store them on your computer's hard drive or an external drive instead.

~

Exercises

Exercise 1:

Find your "Documents" folder *for your hard drive.* It is indented under "This PC" on the left side area in the File Explorer. Pin this folder to quick access. You can do this by right clicking on the folder and selecting "Pin to Quick Access."

Exercise 2:

Find your "Documents" folder *in the cloud.* Save a file to this folder. Note how the file's status changes in the *status* column after you save the file. First, a syncing cloud icon appears, indicating that the file is being uploaded to the cloud. Then a green checkmark appears, meaning that the file is on your computer too, and you can access it even if you are *offline* (not connected to the Internet).

Exercise 3:

Open a web browser, and go to Google Drive. (drive.google.com). Note how much space you are using from your free 15 GB (look on the left-hand side under the folders). Click on the "+ New" icon on the upper left-hand side of the screen, and select "Google Docs." This creates a new Google document. Files in Google Docs are saved every few milliseconds, so there is no need to save the files.

Exercise 4:

Think about where you want to store your files. Decide if you are mainly going to store your files in the cloud or on your hard drive. This does not have to be an all-or-nothing decision. You can store some files in the cloud and some on your hard drive. The key is to be intentional and systematic about where you store your files, so you can find them again later.

Chapter 8: Online Banking and the HTTPS Protocol

In this chapter, we discuss online banking and the https protocol.

Online Banking

Most commercial banks and utility companies have websites that allow you to pay your bills online with an electronic check or money transfer. Most also allow you to pre-set a payment for a specific amount on a particular day each time. For example, you can set up a bill to always be paid on the twenty-fifth of each month, on a specific day of the week, every week, every two weeks, and so on. Using this kind of service means you don't have to remember to send a check to pay a bill; the bank's online system will take care of it for you. I have used these services for more years than I can remember and have not had any problems with them.

In addition to bank websites, you can keep information about all of your financial accounts in software that you purchase and load onto your computer. The two most commonly used personal financial software applications are Microsoft Money and Quicken. Both applications allow you to accept downloaded transactions from your bank. You can download either directly into the software or to a specially formatted file that you input into the software. Both methods are relatively easy to understand and perform. Once you've done it a couple of times, it will come naturally to you.

HTTPS Protocol

One thing that should be mentioned here is the security of the banks' website, and for that matter, any site that expects you to enter personal or credit card/banking information. The way you will know if the site is secure is to look at the web address. It will begin with "https" instead of "http." You also will see a little closed lock 🔒 near the far left side of the browser's address bar. An https protocol for a website means your data is sent encrypted between your computer and the server behind the website. This way, if anyone intercepts the data, they can't read it because they won't be able to decrypt it, as the encryption is based on the connection between the server and your computer. A deeper discussion of encryption is beyond the scope of this book.

> **Note**: Be sure to practice good security when making online transactions.

Security Tip: If you make or plan to make a lot of Internet purchases, I recommend obtaining a separate credit card that you can use solely for online purchases. Also, make sure the credit card has a low credit limit, such as $300 or $500 because even though you may practice good security measures, sometimes your card information may be stolen from the company from which you are making the transaction. If your credit card information gets stolen and used, you are not legally liable for the charges, and the credit card companies will remove the fraudulent charges from your account. Finally, I don't recommend using a debit card online because if your debit card information gets stolen, you will have to set up all of your autopay bills from your bank when you're issued a new account.

Exercises

Exercise 1:

Pick a credit card that you own. Look at your statement, and find its Internet address.

- Go to that address and sign up for an account.
- Pay your bill online.

Exercise 2:

Select a utility bill. Look at your monthly statement, and find the Internet address where you can pay your bill.

- Go to that address, and register for a new account.
- Sign up for autopay. This means that funds will automatically be drafted from your bank account to pay your bill on or near the due date.

Chapter 9: Security

In this chapter, we discuss the dark side of the Internet. We begin with a discussion of basic security terminology and how to protect your computer. Then we delve into email protection and how to spot a scam.

The Dark Side of the Internet

Like anything, the Internet can be used for good or evil. Below are some keywords that come up in any discussion of the dark side of the Internet.

Vocabulary

Virus – This is a type of *malware* that, when executed, replicates by inserting copies of itself (possibly modified) into other computer programs, data files, or the boot sector of a computer's hard drive. The affected areas are then said to be "infected." Viruses often perform some type of harmful activity on infected hosts, such as stealing hard disk space or CPU time, accessing private information, corrupting data, displaying political or humorous messages on the user's screen, spamming their contacts, or logging their keystrokes. However, not all viruses carry a destructive payload or attempt to hide themselves. The defining characteristic of viruses is that they are self-replicating computer programs that install themselves without the user's consent.

Malware – This is a general term used to refer to a variety of forms of hostile, intrusive, or malicious software. Such software is used to disrupt computer operations, gather sensitive information, or gain access to private computer systems. It can appear in the form of code, scripts, active content, and other software.

Worm - A computer worm is a standalone malware program that replicates itself and spreads to other computers. Often, it uses a computer network to spread itself, relying on security failures on the target computer to access it. Unlike a computer virus, worms don't need to attach themselves to an existing program. Worms almost always cause at least some harm to the network, even if only by consuming bandwidth, whereas viruses almost always corrupt or modify files on a targeted computer.

Trojan Horse – This is a non-self-replicating type of malware program containing malicious code that, when executed, typically causes loss or theft of data and possible harm to the system. The term "Trojan horse" is derived from the story of the wooden horse used to trick defenders of Troy into taking concealed warriors into their city in ancient Anatolia. Similar to the Greek warriors in the story, Trojans often employ a form of social engineering, presenting themselves as routine, useful, or interesting, in order to persuade victims to install them on their computers.

A Trojan horse often acts as a backdoor, contacting a controller that can then have unauthorized access to the affected computer. The Trojan and backdoors are not easily detectable, but if they carry out significant computing or communications activity, they may cause the computer to run slowly. Malicious programs are classified as Trojans if they don't attempt to inject themselves into other files (computer virus) or otherwise propagate themselves (worm). A computer may host a Trojan via a malicious program that a user is duped into downloading and executing (often an e-mail attachment disguised to be unsuspicious, e.g., a routine form to be filled in).

Spyware – Spyware is software that aids in gathering information about a person or organization without their knowledge and which may send such information to another entity without the user's consent. It may also assert control over a computer without the user's knowledge.

Spyware is mostly classified into four types: system monitors, Trojans, adware, and tracking cookies. Spyware is mostly used for tracking and storing Internet users' movements on the web and serving up pop-up ads.

Rootkit – A rootkit is a stealthy type of software that is typically malicious and is designed to hide the existence of certain processes or programs from normal methods of detection and enable continued privileged access to a computer. The term "rootkit" is a concatenation of "root" (the traditional name of the privileged account on Unix operating systems) and "kit" (the software components that implement the tool). The term "rootkit" has negative connotations through its association with malware.

Phishing – Phishing is the act of attempting to acquire sensitive information such as usernames, passwords, and credit card details (and sometimes, indirectly, money) by masquerading as a trustworthy entity in an electronic communication. Communications purporting to be from popular social networking websites, auction sites, banks, online payment processors, or IT administrators are commonly used to lure the unsuspecting public. Phishing emails may contain links to websites that are infected with malware. Phishing is typically carried out by email spoofing or instant messaging, and it often directs users to enter details at a fake website whose look and feel are almost identical to the legitimate one. Phishing is an example of social engineering techniques used to deceive users and exploit poor security of current web technologies. Attempts to deal with the growing number of reported phishing incidents include legislation, user training, public awareness, and technical security measures.

Vishing – Vishing is the act of calling individuals and claiming to be from a trustworthy company in order to trick that individual into revealing sensitive personal information.

Whaling - Whaling is a phishing attack that targets high-profile employees, such as the chief executive officer of a company, in order to steal sensitive information from that company.

Adware - Adware is software designed to fill your computer screen with advertisements, especially in a web browser.

Virus Protection Software

As you can see, it is important to protect yourself from harmful software. A good way to do this is by purchasing an antivirus program. Some of the most popular antivirus protection programs are:

- Webroot Secure Anywhere
- Norton Antivirus
- Bitdefender Antivirus Plus
- McAfee Antivirus Plus
- Malwarebytes

Passwords

It's important that you create passwords that are difficult for hackers (including friends and family) to guess.

Security Tip: Don't use the same password for every online account you have, especially for banking. Although it is easy to remember passwords this way, it means that if the password is compromised, hackers will have access to every online account that you have, including your online banking accounts.

Password Generators

Most browsers have a password support feature that will suggest a strong password for you when you sign up for a website. You can take these suggestions, or you can create your own.

Creating Your Own Passwords

I recommend creating a password that is twelve to sixteen characters long. Be sure to use a combination of letters, including capital and lower-case letters, numbers, and symbols (e.g., $&#@!*^%). One trick is to create a sentence and take the first letter of every word in the sentence. For example, you can create the sentence "I love learning about computers and taking classes at the Forever Learning Institute." Taking the first letter of each word, we have "illacatcatfli." Then capitalize a few letters—iLlaCatcatfLi. Next, change a few characters to symbols, and add a few random characters and numbers, and you have a strong password—iLl@C#t44Cat$Li. Alternatively, you can do a Google search for "password generator."

Remembering Your Passwords

Nearly every website you go to will require you to create an account/login. It is nearly impossible to remember all of the passwords you create.

Every time you create a new account, your next step should be to write down the password.

You can write them on a piece of paper and store them in your filing cabinet or in a desk drawer. You also can use encrypted notes on your smartphone. If you search the app store for "encrypted notes," programs like "Secure Notepad" will come up. You can use one of these programs.

Another way is to keep a list of passwords in a file on your computer. Of course, you'll have to think of an innocuous name for that file, so no one knows what's in it. You can also password protect the file. To learn how to password protect a file, go to google.com and search for "how to password protect a file in Microsoft Word." You'll have to update it every time you add or change a password.

Another way to store your passwords is to use the feature that stores passwords in the browser.

Finally, you can store passwords using a digital password vault application such as Bitwarden or Lastpass. You will have to go to their website and download their application. They are fairly easy to use.

Email Fraud

Email fraud is intentional deception made for personal gain or to damage another individual through email. Almost as soon as email became widely used, it was used as a means to defraud people. Email fraud can take the form of a con game or scam. Con games tend to exploit the inherent greed and dishonesty of their victims. The prospect of a bargain or "something for nothing" can be tempting. Email fraud, as with other "bunco schemes," usually targets naive individuals who put their confidence in get-rich-quick schemes such as "too good to be true" investments or offers to sell popular items at impossibly low prices. Many people have lost their life savings due to fraud.

An example scam email

From: Lisa Webbiu lwebbiu05@gmail.com
Subject: Regarding: your new subscription renewal confirmation"
Date: February 6, 2023 at 10:49 AM
To: undisclosed-recipients:;

Thanks

Geek SQUAD

DATE : 02-06-2023

Your Subscription with GEEK SQUAD will Renew Today and $419.00 is about to be Debite from your account by Today. The Debited Amount will be reflected within the next 24.
In case of any further clarifications or block the auto-renewal service please reach out Customer Help Center +1 (808) 658-8753

Customer ID	59065674303674
Invoice Number	GRS8320JS730
Quantity	(One Year Subscription)
Subtotal	$419.00
Sales Tax	$0.00
Total	$419.00

If you didn't authorize this Charge, you have 24 Hrs. To cancel & get an instant refund of your annual subscription, please contact our customer care: +1 (808) 658-8753

You're receiving this mail as you've registered on the Best Buy App & subscribed t our communication updates.

Digitally Yours ,
Team BEST BUY,
Customer support : +1 (808) 658-8753

Figure 14: An example scam email

Security Tip: Several important clues will tip you off that an email is a scam. First, note that a real business will have perfect grammar in its emails. Therefore, if you receive an email with broken English, improper capitalization, or incorrect punctuation, it is most likely a scam. A second way to spot scams is to look at the "From" field of the email. If the email is from a legitimate company, it will have an email address that is from that company. For example, an email from Discover Card will be from dontrply@services.discovercard.com. It has the company name in the email address itself. It will *not* come from a gmail account. Third, legitimate companies will generally address you by your first name, although sometimes, they will use a formal last name greeting (e.g., Mr. Smith). If your email has a general salutation, such as "Dear Customer" or "Dear <your_email_address>," it is likely a scam. Fourth, if an email wants immediate action for something—for example, they claim that they will close your account if you don't call them right away—it is likely a scam. Finally, look at the "To" field of the email. If it goes to "undisclosed recipients" addresses, it is a scam. If you spot a scam, don't open any attachments, click on any links, or call any associated phone numbers. Just delete the email, then don't give it a second thought.

Remember: if it sounds too good to be true, it probably is.

If You Are the Victim of an Online Scam

If you are the victim of an online scam, you may want to report the scam to the FBI's Internet Crime Complaint Center (IC3), which is located at https://www.ic3.gov/.

~

Exercises

Exercise 1:

See if you can identify why the email in Figure 14 is a scam. The answer to this question is at the end of the book.

Exercise 2:

Go through your passwords, and change all the passwords that you use more than once.

Exercise 3:

Take a few moments to answer this question: how would you feel if someone hacked into your computer and had access to all your computer files, or if someone hacked into your bank account and was able to steal money from you?

Exercise 4:

Open a web browser, and go to https://www.ic3.gov/. Click on "File a Complaint" in the top menu bar. Look at the various options you have if you are the victim of a cyber crime.

Ongoing Exercise

Use strong passwords, and write them down in a special place. Replace all of your weak passwords with strong ones.

Chapter 10: Privacy

In this chapter, we discuss online and computer privacy. We also discuss cookies, how they can harm your computer and disturb your privacy, and what to do with them.

Websites

Online privacy is important. Many companies collect data on you when you use their website or their applications. New laws are coming out about your data, what companies can do with data they collect from you, and how you can manage your data (e.g., delete your data from the companies database). For example, Google stores your search history. If you want to change how much information and what kinds of information Google stores about you, go to google.com, click on your profile icon in the upper-right-hand corner, and then go to "Manage your Google Account." You will see several options under Data & Privacy.

Tip: If you want more privacy when you browse, most browsers will include a private mode or an *incognito mode.* Incognito mode is usually under the "File" menu. When in incognito mode, the browser won't save your browsing history, your cookies or site data, information you entered in forms, and miscellaneous permissions that you give to websites. However, incognito mode still allows some websites to view your browsing activity. Therefore, your activity, like your location, might still be visible to websites you visit, including the ads and resources used on those websites, websites you sign in to, your employer, school, or whoever runs the network you are using, your Internet service provider, and search engines. Search engines use location data and activity to show search suggestions based on your location. Additional information that might still be visible include your IP address and your identity when you sign in to a web service, such as Gmail. Finally, any websites that you bookmark or any files that you download are still stored in incognito mode as well.

Social Media

Social media also collects data on you. It is important to check your privacy settings in your social media. (see Chapter 11: Social Media)

Games

Games, especially mobile games and games on social media, collect vast amounts of information on you. If you would like to learn more and your rights concerning the data they collect, I recommend reading the terms of service agreement for each website/game.

Cookies

Cookies are small text files that are stored on your computer. The server behind the website uses them to communicate with your computer and store information such as your username and login info, website preferences, and the place on the website that you left off at, and what's in your shopping cart. This allows the website to streamline your website experience. For instance, it will remember your preferences, pick up where you left off when you return to a website, or remember what is in your shopping cart if you accidentally leave or close the web page. Additional types of cookies are cookies track you as you surf across websites.

When you go to a website, you will often see a banner at the bottom of the page that says something to the effect of "We use cookies to make your experience of our website better. By using and further navigating this website, you accept this." Most of the time, you only have one option—to accept cookies. Generally, I accept cookies on a website. Sometimes you will have the option to decline cookies. If that option is available, I decline them. The disadvantage to declining cookies is that sometimes a website won't work unless cookies are enabled.

Why Cookies Can Be Dangerous

Cookies, in and of themselves, are not malicious. They can't infect your computer with viruses or other malware. However, some cyberattacks can hijack cookies and gain access to your browsing sessions. They can also install adware and spyware into your browser. When this happens, third parties can gain access to your browsing history and personal data that is stored in the web browser cookies. Some virus protectors protect against these kinds of cyberattacks.

How to Delete Cookies

Cookies take up space on your hard drive. They can be removed without any worry about doing harm to your computer. In fact, it is good to clear your cookie history occasionally. Most browsers allow you to do this by going to Settings -> Privacy and Security -> Clear Browsing History. This will be slightly different in each browser.

~

Exercises

Exercise 1:

Read the privacy policy for Facebook. It can be found here: https://www.facebook.com/privacy/policy.

Exercise 2:

Clear the cookies from your browser.

Chapter 11: Social Media

In this chapter, we discuss social media. We begin with what social media is. Then we discuss common social media platforms. Finally, we conclude with a short discussion on blogging.

What Is Social Media?

Social media is a collection of online tools that enable you to keep in touch with friends and other online users throughout the world. Examples of social media include Facebook, X (formerly Twitter), Pinterest, Flicker, Instagram, YouTube, and TikTok.

Facebook

What Can I Do on Facebook?

On Facebook, you can connect with friends, post updates about yourself, create a timeline, which is basically a history of your life, create "stories," and get updates on friends as well. The URL for Facebook is www.facebook.com.

You can also join Facebook groups, which are Facebook pages dedicated to a particular organization. For example, the Forever Learning Institute's Facebook page is https://www.facebook.com/ForeverLearningInstitute.org/.

Recently, Facebook has been rebranded as Meta. You can still use the facebook.com URL and refer to it as Facebook. However, keep an eye out for changes in the future.

Where Do I Start?

The first thing you want to do is check out your privacy options. This sets the system up so that only people you want to can see certain things about you. Access the privacy settings by going to your profile icon in the upper-right-hand corner of the page and selecting "Settings and Privacy" and then "Privacy Checkup." From there, go to "who can see what you share." I recommend that you keep your email address and all of your information so that only your friends can see it. Otherwise, everything you post is accessible to the entire world on the web.

Next, you want to find friends. Facebook will take a guess at which people you know when you first sign up or log in. Otherwise, you can search for and invite people to be your friends. Just as you can make someone your friend, you can also unfriend someone if you wish. You can follow people and organizations as well, which means that updates to their page are pushed to your newsfeed, so you don't have to go to that person or organization's feed to get updates.

Facebook also includes an instant chat program called Messenger, which enables you to send messages privately to your friends.

> **Security Tip**: if you get a friend request for a person who is already your friend (with the exact same name), that is a scammer trying to get into your profile. Don't accept any duplicate friend requests, especially on Messenger!

Overview

On your home screen, you will see your "wall." A wall is like a virtual wall where you can write/post information and where you can see what your friends are posting. You can see other individuals' walls as well. A post is a short sentence or two that you want to share with your friends or with the world (depending on your privacy settings). You can also add pictures or videos to posts. You can "like," "dislike," and "love" posts. You can comment on posts, including other individual's posts as well.

You can also create "stories" and "reels." A story is a couple of pictures about an event . Stories are only visible for twenty-four hours, but you can always revisit stories that you've shared in your story archive.

Next, you might want to follow some groups. Click on "discover" to find a group. Then click on "join group."

The next thing that you'll want to do is update your profile. To do this, click on your picture in the upper-left-hand corner of the page. You can customize your profile photograph and add a background picture as well. Also, click on the "About" section to add more details.

You can chat with people on the lower bottom of the screen in the Messenger program. You can even chat from your cell phone in Messenger.

For people who input their birthdays, Facebook tells you when other individual's birthdays are. It usually will send you an email, and then you can leave a birthday message on their wall. It is an especially nice thing on your friends and family's birthdays or special anniversaries.

You can also play many games on Facebook. Most of these games are free to play, but be careful! If you read the privacy notices, it says that the game creators can collect any and all information about you. Another drawback to playing these games is that they inundate you with ads.

X (formerly Twitter)

X is a social media website in which you can exchange pictures, videos, news, and text with other people. You communicate with other people via "posts," "reposts," and "quotes." A post may contain photos, videos, links, and up to 280 characters of text. There is also an option to create a longer post. X is still located at the URL twitter.com.

What Can I Do on X?

You can make posts, follow people, and comment on posts.

Where Do I Start?

Start with the settings, and ensure that your profile information is private unless you want your photos and videos to be visible to the entire world.

Overview

People are referred to by the @ symbol. e.g., @cynthia_nikolai. Threads are usually denoted by a hashtag (#).

Pinterest

Pinterest is a social media platform that allows you to "pin" videos and images on a wall. Think of this like your story in pictures. A lot of people use Pinterest display artwork or to collect images of items. For example, you can create a collection of images of poses of people that you would like to draw. The address for Pinterest is www.pinterest.com.

Where do I start?

The first thing you'll want to do is check out privacy settings. Ensure that your personal information isn't public.

Overview

On Pinterest, walls are called boards. You create boards to save your "pins" to. What are pins? They are images and videos from the web that you like or that you create yourself. You can download images to your computer and share images on other social media platforms. If you are an artist or a photographer, you can add your art and photography, so others can see your work. Other people can also download your images as well, so make sure you don't share anything that you want to sell or that you don't want the world to see.

Flickr

Flickr enables users to share, organize, and manage their photos online. Users can upload photos and videos to share with friends and followers. One special feature of Flickr is that you can give your friends, family, and other contacts permission to organize your digital media. Your friends, family, and contacts can also add comments, notes and tags to the media.

Where Do I Start?

The first thing you'll want to do is check out your privacy settings. Ensure that your personal information isn't public.

Instagram

Instagram is another social media platform that allows you to share updates with friends and followers. It is owned by Meta, so it is similar to Facebook, but it doesn't have nearly as many features. Again, you can share images and videos and "like" them as well.

A lot of people use Instagram to display artwork. An example of a wall that someone created is Chris Anderson's page at https://www.instagram.com/chrisandersoncma/.

Where Do I Start?

As usual, start with the settings and ensure that your profile information is private unless you want your photos and videos to be visible to the entire world.

TikTok

TikTok is a social media platform that is based around videos. You can upload videos, and like all social media, you can follow people as well. TikTok is located at TikTok.com.

Where Do I Start?

Start with the settings and ensure that your profile information is private unless you want your video to be visible to the entire world.

Blogging

Blogs are personal websites or web pages on which an individual records opinions, links to other sites, and so forth on a regular basis. An example of a free blogging site is www.blogger.com, but many other blogging sites are available. Just search "create your own blog."

> **Note**: For each of these social media websites, you can download an accompanying phone and tablet app as well.

~

Exercises

Exercise 1:

1. Create a Facebook account.
2. Check the privacy settings, and ensure they are what you want them to be. You can do this by clicking on your profile picture in the upper-right-hand corner. Then go to Settings and Privacy → Privacy Checkup.
3. Search for a high school friend in the search bar. Send them a friend request.
4. Create a post.
5. Create a "story."
6. Join a Facebook group.
7. Follow a person or organization.

Exercise 2:

1. Create an X account.
2. Check the privacy settings, and ensure they are what you want them to be.
3. Create an X post.
4. Follow another person.

Exercise 3:

1. Create a Pinterest account.
2. Check the privacy settings, and ensure they are what you want them to be.
3. Go to google.com, search for a picture, and pin that picture to a board.

Exercise 4:

1. Create a Flickr account.
2. Check the privacy settings in Flickr.
3. Create a photo album.

Exercise 5:

1. Create an Instagram account.
2. Check the privacy settings, and ensure they are what you want them to be.
3. Upload a picture of your choice to a board.

Exercise 6:

1. Create a TikTok account.
2. Check the privacy settings, and ensure they are what you want them to be.
3. Create and post a video.

Exercise 7:

Choose 1 option:

1. Open a web browser, go to Google, and search for "free blogging platforms." Choose one platform, and explore it.
2. Go to www.blogger.com, and explore it.

Did you know? You can create a free website on www.wordpress.com or www.sites.google.com.

Chapter 12: Backup and Recovery Concepts

In this chapter, we discuss what data to back up, when to back up your data, and how to back up your data.

Overview

In information technology, a backup, or the process of backing up, refers to the copying and archiving of computer data, so it can be used to restore the original after a data-loss event. The verb form is "back up" in two words, whereas the noun is "backup."

Backups have two distinct purposes. The primary purpose is to recover data after its loss, be it by data deletion or corruption. Data loss can be a common experience for computer users. A 2021 survey found that 62 percent of respondents had lost data at some point. The secondary purpose of backups is to recover data from an earlier time, according to a user-defined data retention policy, typically configured within a backup application. Though backups represent a simple form of disaster recovery and should be part of a disaster-recovery plan, by themselves, backups alone should not be considered disaster recovery. One reason for this is that not all backup systems or backup applications are able to reconstitute a computer system.

Since a backup system contains at least one copy of all data worth saving, the data storage requirements can be significant. Organizing this storage space and managing the backup process can be a complicated undertaking. A data-repository model can be used to provide structure to the storage. Nowadays, many different types of data-storage devices are useful for making backups. These devices can be arranged in many different ways to provide geographic redundancy, data security, and portability.

Before data is sent to its storage location, it is selected, extracted, and manipulated. Many different techniques have been developed to optimize the backup procedure. These include optimizations for dealing with open files and live data sources as well as compression, encryption, and de-duplication, among others. Every backup scheme should include dry runs that validate the reliability of the data being backed up. The limitations and human factors involved in any backup scheme should be recognized.

What to Back Up

You will want to back up all data files that you have updated recently. If you purchase a commercial backup system, it will do an initial backup of all of your files. Incremental backups (backups of only files that have changed since your last backup) will be done on a schedule that you specify.

When to Back Up

How often you back up your files depends on how much you are willing to recreate when some type of file corruption occurs. Take into account whether or not backup can be done (i.e., data will be permanently lost or recaptured from its source) if the data isn't backed up. Typically, a backup should be scheduled on a daily basis at a time you are not using the computer. You will need to ensure that the computer is turned on at that time of day.

How to Back Up

You can opt to back up files yourself using an external drive, or you can use a commercial backup system, such as Carbonite.

To back up your computer to an external drive, you will have to purchase an external drive or a USB (a.k.a. thumb) drive. You can purchase one at Best Buy, Office Max/Depot, Staples, or online at a site like Amazon. To back up your computer, connect the drive to your computer and then copy the files that you would like to back up to the external drive. A good philosophy to remember when backing up is three, two, one. This means that you should have three backups of your data, two of which are on different types of media systems (e.g., external drive and a USB drive), and one of which is in a different physical location than the other two.

I recommend using a commercial backup system because, otherwise, you have to determine what files have changed on your computer since your last backup. This can be difficult to determine, and you may end up backing up more than you need to, thereby using more external disk space. It also can be confusing as to which files are the most current versions of your data. Finally, commercial software comes with automatic backup scheduling, so you don't have to remember to back things up.

~

Exercises

Exercise 1:
Ponder the following question: how would you feel if you lost all of your computer files? What steps can you take now to ensure that you are backing up your files?

Exercise 2:
Decide how you are going to back up your files (e.g., in the cloud, on an external drive, or on a commercial backup system). Decide what files you are going to back up, then create a schedule for backing up your files.

Exercise 3:
Back up your files right now.

Chapter 13: Frequently Asked Questions

What's the difference between "save" and "save as"?

You will select "save" when you have a new document that you have never saved before, and you want to store it on your computer. Save it to your hard drive in the "Documents" folder or in the cloud (e.g., OneDrive).

You will also select "save" when you have changes that you make to the document, and you want to save those changes to your hard drive.

You will select "save as" when you want to make a copy of the document that you have open already. This saves a copy of the document under a new name.

What's the difference between "upload" and "download"?

"Upload" is when you push information out from your computer to some other computer or server. "Download" is when you pull information from another computer or server onto your computer. You can upload to and download from the cloud.

Oops, I deleted my file. Now what?

When you delete a file, it's not really gone. It goes into the "Recycle Bin," also known as "Trash" on Apple computers. The Recycle Bin is a small space that holds files that have been deleted. You can retrieve files from the Recycle Bin and put them back into your File Explorer (right click on the item in the Recycle Bin and select "restore"). Files in your Recycle Bin still take up space on your computer. Therefore, every once and a while you will want to empty your Recycle Bin or Trash. When you empty your Recycle Bin, the files are permanently deleted from your computer.

My computer has served its life, and it is time to get a new one. How do I "clean" my computer?

Before you get rid of your old computer, you will want to back up your old files. You can either save the files to a cloud, such as OneDrive or Google Drive, or you can copy them to an external drive, such as a USB drive. Once that is complete, you can "migrate" your files from your old computer to your new computer. Your new computer will have a "migration assistant" to help you migrate between computers. Next, you will want to erase your old hard drive and all the data on it, so no one can get ahold of your old files. You can erase your hard drive by going to Settings -> System -> Recovery and click "Reset PC." When asked what you want to erase, select "Remove everything." Finally, you will want to dispose of your old computer. You can take your computer to a store like Best Buy, and they will recycle it for you for free. It is good to recycle your old computer as opposed to throwing it away because the various internal parts can be recycled and may have a negative impact on the environment if put in a landfill.

Chapter 14: Where to Go if You Need Help

What to Do if You Have a Virus

If you have a virus on your computer, I recommend taking the computer to Best Buy to the Geek Squad. They have advanced software that they can use to clean your computer. You may also have a local computer store that you can use. Although this does cost money, it is well worth it because once a virus gets into your computer, it will keep replicating and clogging up your computer. Once that happens, your computer will slow down. It can also compromise personal information.

What If I Don't Know How to Do Something On My Computer?

Massive amounts of information are stored on the Internet. I recommend searching with google (www.google.com) as your first step. You can also search through instructional videos on YouTube (www.youtube.com). You can find almost any answer to your question on these two websites.

Still Stuck?

I'm available to answer questions, no matter how big or how small. I can answer questions about Windows, Macs, and Chromebooks as well as questions about Android and Apple tablets and cell phones. You can contact me at cnikolai01@gmail.com or 240-645-7660. We can discuss pricing, depending on the scope of the problem/question at hand.

Like This Book?

I would love to hear from you. Shoot me an email at cnikolai01@gmail.com. I would also love it if you could leave me a review on Amazon or Google.

Chapter 15: Common Computer Vocabulary

adware – software designed to fill your computer screen with advertisements, especially in a web browser.

antivirus software – a program that finds and removes viruses from a computer.

application – software that operates on a personal computer and does various things, such as word-processing, accounting, and creating graphics. Applications can also exist on a server.

AWS – short for "Amazon Web Services." It mostly is used by commercial companies, small businesses, and web developers.

backup – a copy of files from a computer's hard disk, usually made on an external medium such as a CD-ROM, DVD, or flash drive, or stored in the cloud. A backup is made in case the hard disk file(s) are erased or damaged.

bit, byte – a bit is the smallest piece of information that computers use. For simplicity, a personal computer (PC) uses bits in groups of eight, and they are called bytes (eight bits = one byte).

blog – a personal website or web page on which an individual records opinions, links to other sites, and so forth on a regular basis.

bluetooth – a way of communicating wirelessly over short distances between electronic devices (for example computer and mobile telephone).

boot, boot up, boot disk – You boot (or boot up) your computer when you switch it on and wait while it prepares itself. Instructions for startup are given to the computer from the boot disk, which is usually the hard disk.

browser, to browse – A browser is a program like Firefox, Chrome, Safari, DuckDuckGo, or Edge. You use it to view web pages or to browse the Internet.

bug – a (small) defect or fault in a program.

cache – a kind of memory used to make a computer work faster.

client – a computer that communicates with a server. You—or more accurately, your computer—are the client.

cookie – information stored on your computer by websites that is sent between your computer and a website to remember personal information such as your username and what's in your shopping cart.

CD-ROM – a disk for storing computer information. It looks like an audio CD.

CPU – short for "central processing unit." This is a PC's "heart" or "brain."

data – the information (e.g., text, pictures, audio) that you create or share on a computer.

desktop – a computer that sits on top of (or under) your desk. Unlike a laptop or notebook, a desktop is usually not portable. Desktops are usually made in the form of a small "tower" to hold the computer components.

downloading – the act of saving a file stored on a server/ website onto your computer, tablet, or phone.

driver – a small program that tells a PC how a peripheral works.

DVD – a disk for storing computer information. It looks like a CD, but it can store more information than a CD.

eBook – an electronic book that can be downloaded and read on a computer or other electronic device.

electronic mail (email, e-mail) – messages sent from one computer to another. You can read email on the screen or print it out.

email fraud – intentional deception of an individual via email for the purpose of personal gain or to inflict damage on another person.

emoji – a cute little icon, such as a smiley face, that is sent in a text message or email.

file – a specific computer record used to store data. Files contain data such as text (e.g., essay.docx), or a program (e.g., paint.exe). Files are kept in folders. Files are also called documents.

flash drive – a portable disk for storing computer information. See *USB flash drive.*

folder (directory) – a sub-division of a computer's hard disk into which you put files.

font – a specialized type of lettering on the screen or on paper. Fonts are classified into *serif*, where letters contain little tails on them, or *sans serif*, where letters don't have any tails on them. "Arial" is a kind of font, and it looks like this. Arial is a sans serif font. "Times New Roman" is another type of font, and it looks like this. Times New Roman is a serif font.

format – all hard disks and floppy disks must be electronically prepared for use by a process called formatting. Hard disks are pre-formatted by the manufacturer. If you buy a disk that is not pre-formatted, you must format it yourself, using a program that comes with your PC.

forum – a virtual space or set of web pages where ideas and views on a particular issue can be exchanged.

freeware – software that is free to use (doesn't require you to purchase it).

graphics card – the equipment inside a computer that creates images on the screen.

hard disk/hard drive – the main disk inside a computer used for storing programs and information. It is hard because it is metal. Currently, there are two common types of hard drives—hard disk drives (HDDs) and solid state drives (SSDs). SSDs are the latest type of hard drive technologies available.

hotspot – an area that has an available wireless signal for Internet access (usually public).

http – short for hypertext transfer protocol. This is the standard set of rules for how to format and transfer data across the web. Data transmitted through http are transmitted in plain text, or unencrypted, between the client (you) and the server (the web page you are accessing).

https – short for "hypertext transfer protocol secure." This is a secure way to format and transfer data across the web. Data transmitted through https are encrypted between the client (you) and the server (the web page you are accessing).

icon – a small image or picture on a computer screen that is a symbol for files, folders, disks, peripherals, and other programs.

Internet – the international network of computers that you connect to by telephone line or fiber optic cable. Two popular services of the Internet are the world wide web and electronic mail.

Internet Service Provider (ISP) – a company that provides a way for users to connect to the Internet. Such companies include AT&T, Comcast/Xfinity, and satellite dish systems.

IP Address – a numerical label assigned to each device connected to a computer network. It uniquely identifies the computer on the Internet. There are two types of addresses—IP version 4 and IP version 6. An example of an IPv4 address is 127.255.304.933. An example of a IPv6 address is 2001:0db8:85a3:0000:0000:8a2e:0370:7334.

iPad – a tablet created by Apple.

KB, MB, GB, TB, PB, EB, ZB – kilobytes, megabytes, gigabytes, terabytes, petabytes, exabytes, zettabytes. A Unit of memory. A kilobyte is 2^{10} = 1,024 bytes or roughly 1000 bytes. A megabyte is 2^{20} = 1,048,576 bytes, or roughly one million bytes. A gigabyte is 2^30 = 1,073,741,824 bytes or roughly one billion bytes. A terabyte 2^40 = 1,099,511,627,776 or roughly 1 trillion bytes. A petabyte is 2^50 = 1,125,899,906,842,624 bytes. An exabyte is 2^60 = 1,152,921,504,606,846,976 bytes. A zettabyte is 2^70 = 1,180,591,620,717,411,303,424 bytes.

Kindle – a device for downloading and reading ebooks. Kindle was developed by Amazon.

"Like" – a feeling that you can attribute to images, videos, or other social media messages, indicating that you like the content. It is usually denoted by a thumbs-up symbol.

Malware – short for "malicious software," malware is used to disrupt computer operations, gather sensitive information, or gain access to private computer systems.

man-in-the-middle attack – a type of attack in which a hacker positions himself/herself in between the initiating point and the destination point. The hacker intercepts and reads the communication from the initiating point and then relays this information to the end point as if nothing happened. In the process, the hacker steals your personal information.

memory – memory is used to store information on a computer. There are two types of memory—permanent and temporary. Permanent memory is saved on a hard drive. Temporary memory is saved in RAM. See also *hard disk, RAM, ROM,* and *cache.*

MHz, GHz – Megahertz, Gigahertz. This describes the speed of the central processing unit. The higher the MHz or GHz, the better the CPU's performance.

modem – a device connected to a computer that's used for sending and receiving digital information by telephone line or fiber optic cable. You may need a modem to connect to the Internet, to send electronic mail, and to send a fax.

multi-factor authentication (MFA) – authentication that requires more than one form of authentication to log into a system. For example, first you enter your username and password, and second, you get a code through your email or a text message on your phone that enables you to fully log in. See also *two-factor authentication.*

notebook – a folding, portable computer, a.k.a. a laptop.

OCR – an abbreviation for "optical character recognition." OCR lets a PC read a fax or scanned image and convert it to actual letters.

one-time password (OTP) – a code that is sent through email or via text message with a password that is valid for one login to the system or application.

open-source software – software whose source code (the code underlying the program itself) is "released" (open to the public). These programs usually are free to use but have qualifications on using them for commercial, educational, and personal uses.

operating system (OS) – The basic software that manages a computer (for example, Windows 10, Windows 11, OS X, Unix, iOS).

parallel port – a socket at the back of a computer for connecting external equipment or peripherals, especially printers.

PC – abbreviation for Personal Computer. Traditionally, this refers to a Windows computer.

phishing – the act of attempting to acquire sensitive information, such as usernames, passwords, and credit card details (and sometimes, indirectly, money) by masquerading as a trustworthy entity in an electronic communication.

peripheral – any equipment that is connected externally to a computer. Printers, scanners, and keyboards are peripherals.

pixel – the smallest unit that comprises the image that you see on the screen. It is made of thousands of tiny dots or pixels.

podcast – The Internet equivalent of a radio program. Episodes can range from a few minutes to hours in length. Podcasts might include interviews with notable people, special moments in history, imparted wisdom, and storytelling.

program – software that operates on a personal computer and does various things, such as word processing), accounting, and creating graphics. Program can also exist on a server. See also *application.*

QWERTY – the first six letters on English-language keyboards. The first six letters on French-language keyboards are A-Z-E-R-T-Y.

RAM, ROM – two types of memory. RAM (Random Access Memory) is the main memory used while your PC is working. RAM is temporary. ROM (Read Only Memory) is used for information needed by the PC that is only capable of being read by and cannot be changed by the CPU. An example of ROM is a CD-ROM.

ransomware – a computer attack whereby a hacker encrypts your computer files and holds them for ransom. Hackers usually ask for money to unencrypt your files, and often they ask for payment in the form of cryptocurrency.

resolution – the number of dots or pixels per inch (sometimes per centimeter) used to create the screen image.

rootkit – a stealthy type of software, typically malicious, designed to hide the existence of certain processes or programs from normal methods of detection and enable continued privileged access to a computer.

scanner – equipment used to convert paper documents to electronic documents.

search engine – an application that is aware of all the websites on the Internet. It scans the Internet and searches through the content of each web page and then returns the top result to you in a convenient format. There are four main search engines—Google, DuckDuckGo, Yahoo, and Bing.

server – a specialized computer that "serves" or transmits data to or receives data from a client. It can also process the data that it receives.

smartphone – a mobile phone that provides access to the Internet. There are three kinds of smartphones that make up most of the market: iPhone (made by Apple), Pixel (made by Google), and Android (made by everyone else).

social engineering – the act of deceiving a user in order to gain access to his or her computer. This can occur by phone, email, or personal contact.

social media – the name for a kind of application that helps individuals connect with one other over the Internet. Common social media applications include Facebook, X (formerly Twitter), TikTok, Flickr, Pinterest, and Instagram.

source code – the computer code that underlies an application.

spam – irrelevant or inappropriate messages sent on the Internet to a large number of users.

spyware – software that aids in gathering information about a person or organization without their knowledge and that may send such information to another entity without the consumer's consent. It may also seek to assert control over a computer.

streaming – playing a movie or other type of video or music over the Internet. The server breaks a video or audio file into bite-size chunks (packets) and sends (streams) it over the Internet packet by packet to your computer, tablet, or smartphone. The video or audio is stored in the cloud, but the packets are buffered on your computer (saved in small bite-size chunks). Some streaming services give you the option to download the entire file and save it to your hard disk.

surfing – the act of exploring topics of interest on the Internet. Surfing is conducted with a web browser by going from web page to web page.

syncing – the act of synchronizing your data across all of your electronic devices. This means that when you change/add/delete files or emails on one computer or on your smartphone or tablet, your files are changed/added/deleted on all of your devices.

tablet – a mobile computer with a touchscreen only. Tablets can also have peripheral keyboards attached.

tagged – a term frequently used in social media that denotes when another person identifies you in a photo or video.

the cloud – the name for a group of computers connected together that provides a service to a user, typically storing user data. Multiple clouds are available, including Microsoft's OneDrive, Apple's iCloud, Google's Google Drive, and Adobe's Creative Cloud.

Trojan horse – a non-self-replicating type of program containing malicious code that, when executed, carries out actions causing loss or theft of data and possible harm to the system.

tweet – a posting made on the former social networking site X (formerly known as Twitter). A tweet is limited to 280 characters.

two-factor authentication (2FA) – authentication that requires two forms of authentication to log into a system. For example, first you enter your username and password, and second, you get a code through your email or a text message on your phone that enables you to log in. See also *multi-factor authentication.*

uploading – the act of sending a file from your local computer to a server and storing it on in their database, website, or the cloud.

URI – Uniform Resource Identifier. A formal system for uniquely identifying resources. There are two types of URIs: URLs (Uniform Resource Locator) and URNs (Uniform Resource Name).

URL – Uniform Resource Locator. A unique address that identifies the location of a web page on the Internet. URLs typically begin with www. Example addresses include www.google.com and www.amazon.com.

URN – Uniform Resource Name. A formal naming scheme that identifies a resource but doesn't indicate its location or how to access it (e.g., ISBN, ISSN).

USB – universal serial bus. A standardized connection for attaching devices to computers.

USB drive – a small, external device for storing data. It connects through the USB socket in your computer. USB drives are also called thumb drives or flash drives.

virus – a software program that does something harmful to or otherwise disrupts your computer in a negative way.

vishing – the act of calling individuals and claiming to be from a trustworthy company in order to trick that individual into revealing sensitive personal information.

vpn – virtual private network. A VPN connection helps to provide a more secure connection to a company's network and the internet. VPNs encrypt your network traffic and mask your IP address.

whaling – a phishing attack that targets high-profile employees, such as the chief executive officer of a company, in order to steal sensitive information from that company or otherwise gain access to the company's computer system.

Wi-Fi – a system for communicating without wires over a computer network.

Windows – an operating system used by the majority of personal computers (PCs).

World Wide Web, WWW, the Web – one of the services available on the Internet. It lets you access millions of pages through a system of links. Because it is "worldwide," it was originally called the World Wide Web or WWW. See also *Internet.*

worm – a standalone computer program that replicates itself in order to spread to other computers. Often, it uses a computer network to spread itself, relying on security failures on the target computer to access it. Unlike a computer virus, it doesn't need to attach itself to an existing program.

WYSIWIG – **W**hat **Y**ou **S**ee **I**s **W**hat **Y**ou **G**et. With a WYSIWIG program, if you print a document, it looks the same on paper as it does on the screen.

Appendix 1: Answer to Why This Email Is a Scam

1. It is purportedly from Best Buy's Geek Squad, but it comes from a gmail email address.
2. It is addressed to "undisclosed recipients."
3. The grammar isn't perfect. Notice the spelling, capitalization, and punctuation errors.
4. The logo isn't perfect. Note the light brown edges coming out of the lower-right corner of the logo.

From: [illegible]
Subject: [illegible]
Date: February 6, 2023 at 10:49 AM
To: [illegible]

Thanks

DATE : 02-06-2023

Your Subscription with GEEK SQUAD will Renew Today and $419.00 is about to be Debite from your account by Today. The Debited Amount will be reflected within the next 24.
In case of any further clarifications or block the auto-renewal service please reach out Customer Help Center +1 (808) 658-8753

Customer ID	59065674303674
Invoice Number	GRS8320JS730
Quantity	(One Year Subscription)
Subtotal	$419.00
Sales Tax	$0.00
Total	$419.00

If you didn't authorize this Charge, you have 24 Hrs. To cancel & get an instant refund of your annual subscription, please contact our customer care: +1 (808) 658-8753

You're receiving this mail as you've registered on the Best Buy App & subscribed t our communication updates.

Digitally Yours ,
Team BEST BUY,
Customer support : +1 (808) 658-8753

Figure 14: An example scam email

Whatever you do, do *not* call the number given in this email. This is not the Geek Squad's number. If you were to call this number, the people behind it would either ask you for personal information or ask you to download some software onto your computer. The software is malware that will infect your computer and steal your personal information. If you have any doubts at all as to if these are actually your charges, close the email, look up Best Buy's phone number by other means (either Google or a phone book), and call them to ask about the charges. Otherwise, delete this email, and don't give it a second thought.

For the same reason, never open or download any attachment from suspected scam emails.

www.ingramcontent.com/pod-product-compliance
Lightning Source LLC
Chambersburg PA
CBHW050505250125
20805CB00049B/1247

9781038303738